Stories of Freedom

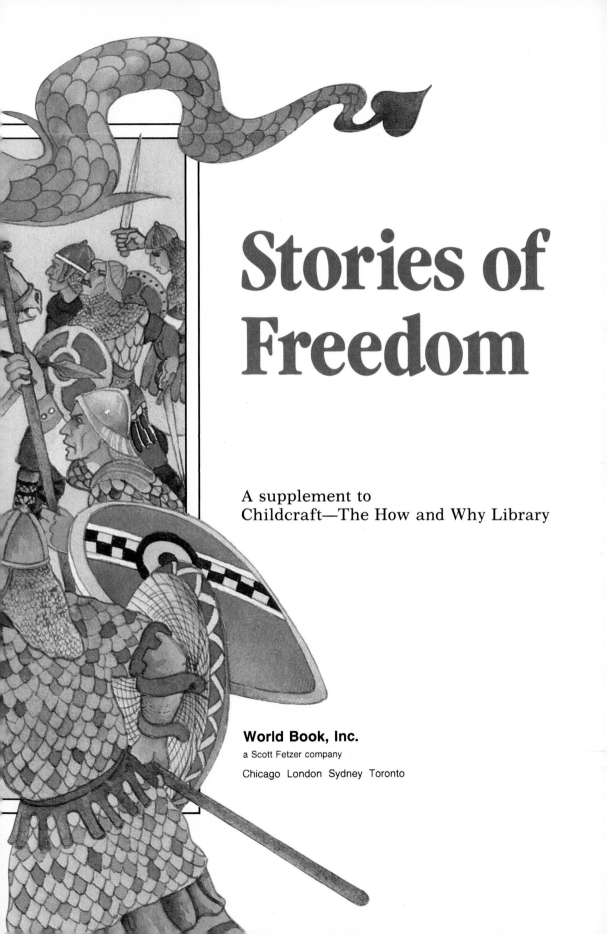

Stories of Freedom

A supplement to
Childcraft—The How and Why Library

World Book, Inc.
a Scott Fetzer company
Chicago London Sydney Toronto

Contents

Editorial Advisory Board

for Childcraft—The How and Why Library

Staff

Preface

War is a terrible thing. And, sadly, most battles and wars don't settle any problems for long. All they do is cause grief and pain and death for many brave people.

But some battles and wars did accomplish something important. In these situations, people were fighting to keep or to gain their freedom. One such war was the American Revolution. Out of that war was born the United States of America, which has been a symbol of freedom ever since. Another was World War II, in which people of many countries fought to prevent Germany, Italy, and Japan from taking over much of the world.

This book tells the stories of fourteen battles in which people fought for their freedom. These stories cover more than three thousand years of history—from the ancient Egyptians who fought to save their land from the destroying horde of the Sea People to the desperate struggle of the British fighter pilots to defend their nation against invasion by Germany.

Here, then, are fourteen stories of courage, heroism, and devotion to the idea of freedom.

The attack of the Sea People

Egypt and Syria
about 1180 B.C.

The Nile River flows through the land of Egypt and into the Mediterranean Sea. But before it reaches the sea, it splits up into a number of wide channels, or streams. One day, more than three thousand years ago, a number of small ships came gliding over the horizon. They sailed into one of the Nile's many channels and headed upstream.

The ships were long and narrow. Each had a single big sail and a high bow, or front, carved into the shape of a bird's head with a long bill. The ships were packed with warriors wearing leather helmets decorated with horns and with circles of feathers.

9

These were the ships and warriors of the mysterious, frightening conquerors known as the "Sea People." They were sailing up the Nile to invade Egypt.

No one knows who these Sea People were or where they came from. But they struck terror into the hearts of people who lived on the shores of the Mediterranean Sea. This vast horde of invaders traveled slowly along the coastline, conquering and destroying. Some of the invaders moved by land, in big two-wheeled carts pulled by oxen. Others moved by sea, in a huge fleet of ships.

On the coast of Greece, the Sea People had attacked and destroyed one city after another. In time, they made their way around the eastern edge of the Mediterranean Sea and entered the countries of the Near East. They moved into the land of the powerful Hittite Empire, which covered most of what is now the nation of Turkey, and wiped it out! The Hittite capital city was completely destroyed, along with smaller towns. A number of small kingdoms along the northern seacoast were crushed.

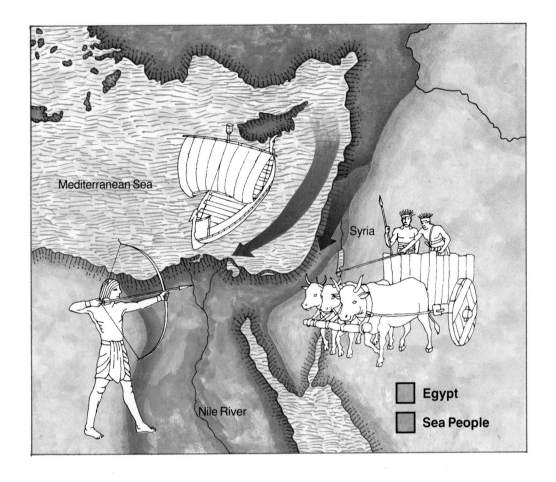

Mediterranean Sea

Syria

Nile River

Egypt

Sea People

Finally, only the ancient land of Egypt stood in the path of this enormous conquering force.

Even at that time, Egypt was an old, old country. It had been a single nation for nearly two thousand years, and was the mightiest empire of the Western world. It had an army, a navy, laws, and a government headed by a ruler known as the pharaoh (FAIR oh). When the Sea

People launched their attack on Egypt, the pharaoh was a man named Ramses (RAM seez).

The Egyptians knew the Sea People were coming. But Ramses was determined that they would not conquer and ruin his country. He quickly began strengthening the army. He also put men to work building special ships for the navy. He sent scouts and spies to watch for the Sea People, and he made plans for fighting them. When the ships of the Sea People came sailing up the Nile channel, Ramses and the Egyptians were ready.

One after another, the invading ships moved into the channel, until they filled it. Steadily, they sailed toward the heart of Egypt. Bulrushes—plants with long, stiff stems that grow as tall or taller than a person—covered the banks of the channel. Seen from the ships, the bulrushes formed a thick jungle on each side of the channel.

Suddenly, from somewhere among the bulrushes, there came the loud, shrill sound of a horn. To the surprise and shock of the Sea People, thousands of men who had been crouching in the bulrushes stood up. They were soldiers of Egypt, hidden there by the orders of Ramses to ambush the Sea People!

The Egyptian soldiers were armed with bows and arrows. They were skilled archers, and the air throbbed with the twanging of bowstrings like the hum of a horde of angry bees. Clouds of arrows sped toward the ships from both sides of the channel. The arrows thudded into the wooden hulls, ripped through the broad sails, and tore into the bodies of the tightly packed warriors. Again and again the Egyptian bowstrings twanged and arrows hissed through the air.

The ships were helpless.
Clustered closely together in
the narrow channel, they could
not turn around to get away.
They could only keep going in
the hope they would soon pass
the archers and the storm of
arrows.

But now scores of Egyptian
river boats, rowed by many
oarsmen, came racing down
the channel. These were

special boats that Ramses had
ordered built. They were filled
with archers, as well as soldiers
armed with swords or axes.

The Egyptian boats darted
among the bigger, slower ships
of the Sea People. The
Egyptian archers on the boats
snapped arrows into the enemy
warriors at close range. Some
of the boats bumped alongside
ships, and Egyptian soldiers
fought their way aboard,

This ancient Egyptian stone carving shows the pharaoh Ramses III fighting one of the Sea People.

showing no mercy. Many of the Sea People's ships were overturned, filling the water with struggling men. Some were hacked with swords and axes as they tried to climb into the Egyptian boats. Those who tried to swim to shore were shot by the Egyptian archers standing in the bulrushes.

And so, the invasion of Egypt from the sea was a complete disaster for the Sea People. The Egyptian ambush had worked perfectly. Most of the ships were sunk, and most of the enemy warriors were killed. The Egyptians lost only a few men.

But the danger was far from over. The huge horde of Sea People moving by land was still approaching Egypt. The battle with that horde would decide Egypt's fate.

Ramses had determined not to fight that battle on Egypt's soil. He would lead his army into the land of Syria, where the Sea People were. He would fight them there, far from the homes and farms of his people. Quickly, the army was supplied with food, quantities of arrows, and other needs. It then set forth along the coastline.

In most ancient nations, a ruler formed an army by simply rounding up a few thousand men and giving them weapons. But the Egyptian army was different, it was a "professional army," as most armies are today. Egyptian soldiers were well-trained, well-equipped, and sure of themselves.

The army was divided into four main groups of five thousand men each. The groups were named after Egyptian gods—Amun, Re, Sutekh, and Ptah. They also had nicknames, such as "the Courageous Bows," and "the Powerful Bows." The bow was the main Egyptian weapon, and the archers were skilled with it. Egyptian bows were about five feet (1.5 meters) long, and could send an arrow a long way, with considerable power.

Besides archers, there were soldiers who carried spears, axes, and swords. The blades and points of these weapons were made of hammered copper or molded bronze, which is a mixture of copper and tin. All soldiers except the archers carried big wooden shields, some painted and some covered with cowhide. Most of the men were bareheaded, barefooted, and wore only a kind of cloth skirt with a flap of stiff leather that hung down the front.

The pride of the Egyptian army was its force of chariots. These were very light, two-wheeled carts pulled by two horses. Each chariot held two soldiers, an archer and the chariot driver. Each chariot was also equipped with a dozen or so light spears carried in containers fastened to the sides of the chariot. Ramses rode in a special chariot covered with glittering armor made of sheets of mixed silver and gold.

Day after day, the Egyptians marched steadily eastward. Out ahead of the main army, a number of chariots scouted for sight of the approaching enemy. On the morning of the twentieth day of

an Egyptian
war chariot

marching, the advance
chariots came hurrying back.
The Sea People had been seen!

The Egyptians shifted into
fighting formation and moved
forward cautiously. Soon, they
could see the Sea People—a
huge crowd with hundreds of
ox-drawn wagons that
stretched across the horizon.
The sound of their movement
was like a steady rumble of
thunder. Many of the Egyptian

soldiers must have felt fear at the sight
of this vast number of invaders.

As for the Sea People, the Egyptian
army must have been a frightening sight.
The Egyptians advanced in formation,
moving to the shrill scream of brass
trumpets. Scores of chariots sped
alongside the marching men. All the
power of the Egyptian Empire was on
proud display.

Both sides knew that this battle meant
complete victory or total defeat and
destruction. The Egyptians were fighting
to keep this horde from reaching their
country and destroying it. The Sea People

warriors were fighting for their survival and the survival of their wives and children who were in the many ox-drawn carts. Their hope was to conquer Egypt and make it their land!

The warriors of the Sea People rushed to the attack, a wild mass of shouting men, armed mainly with bronze swords and round wooden shields. They outnumbered the Egyptian army, and were sure they could defeat it.

But the Sea People had no archers, and the Egyptian army did. The air buzzed with Egyptian arrows, and hundreds of the Sea People warriors went down without ever reaching the Egyptians. From the scores of Egyptian chariots, skillfully driven in and out among the attackers, came more arrows, and spears. By the time the Sea People warriors reached the battle line of the Egyptian army they had lost many men. Now, better training, better weapons, and the confidence of the Egyptian soldiers made a big difference!

In the end, the two-wheeled wagons of the Sea People dotted the brown Syrian plain. They stood pointing in all directions. Some still had oxen yoked to them, some were filled with wailing women and children, others were empty or filled only with dead warriors. The surviving warriors of the Sea People, now prisoners, stood awaiting their fate. They would be marched back to Egypt where they would be taught the Egyptian language and put into the Egyptian army. The women and children would become household servants.

Thus, the long, conquering march of the Sea People, which had destroyed kingdoms and empires, came to an end. The well-trained, professional soldiers of the Egyptian army had kept their country free and saved civilization!

A city against an Empire

The Battle of Marathon
Greece, 490 B.C.

Eleven grim-faced men stood on a hilltop, gazing out over a valley. Tanned, bearded, and muscular, the men all wore helmets and armor that gleamed like gold.

The center of the valley formed a long, narrow plain that stretched away from the hill for a little more than a mile (1.6 kilometers). At the end of the plain was a beach, and beyond the beach sparkled a broad sheet of water—a bay that led out to the sea. It was this beach that held the attention of the men on the hilltop, for a vast army was encamped there. The beach was dotted with tents and aswarm with men and horses.

Scores of wooden ships were pulled up on the sand, half in and half out of the water.

The men on the hilltop were the commanders of an army encamped in the hills above the plain—an army of Greek soldiers from the cities of Athens (ATH ihnz) and Plataea (pluh TEE uh). The soldiers on the beach were invaders. They had come across the sea from the gigantic Persian Empire to conquer the tiny land of Greece.

The difference between Greece and the Persian Empire was like the difference between a cat and an elephant. It would have taken more than a hundred countries the size of Greece to equal the size of the Persian Empire. Stretching more than three thousand miles (4,800 km) across the Near East, it was made up of many countries that Persia had conquered. It held millions of people who spoke many different languages and had different religions and ways of life. And one man, the Persian emperor Darius (duh RY uhs), ruled them all.

But Greece was a tiny country, no more than two hundred miles (322 km) wide. It consisted of a narrow piece of land surrounded on three sides by water and a number of small islands. The people of Greece all spoke the same language, worshiped the same gods, and had much the same way of life. But Greece was not a single nation—each Greek city was the center of a small, independent state. Each state had its own government, its own laws, and even its own army. However, the people of each city-state were fiercely proud to be Greek, and loved their whole country.

The Persian emperor's main reason for attacking Greece was to punish two of its city-states, Athens and Eretria (eh ree TREE uh). They had sent help to a part of his empire that had tried to revolt against him. But his generals also had orders to conquer the whole country after the two

Aegean Sea

Marathon

Greece

Persian Empire

Eretria

Marathon

Athens

cities were destroyed. So, some
twenty-five hundred years ago,
in the year 490 B.C., a great fleet
of six hundred ships set out from
Persia, across the Aegean Sea to
Greece, to begin the conquest.

Their oars rising and falling
in the gray water, the Persian
ships glided toward the Greek
coast. They landed at a point
not far from the city of
Eretria, and the army marched
straight to the city. Like most
Greek cities, Eretria was
protected by a high, thick wall

and strong gates. It managed to keep the Persians out for six days. Then, they got in, killed most of the men, took all the wealth and treasure they could find, dragged off the women and children to be slaves, and burned Eretria down!

A short time later, about half the Persian army went in ships to another part of the coast where there was a flat plain ringed by hills. The plain was called Marathon. It was only a short distance from the other city that was to be punished, Athens.

The Athenians had learned of what had happened to Eretria, and knew they would be attacked next. They held a great meeting in the market place, the broad, open center of the city, to talk about how to defend themselves. They finally decided not to shut themselves up in their city and try to hold out, as the Eretrians had done. Instead, they would march out and attack the Persians when they arrived.

Meanwhile, messengers were sent to other cities, asking for help. But before any help arrived, the Athenians received news of the Persian landing at Marathon.

This ancient stone carving shows the Persian Emperor Darius, who sent his army to invade Greece.

At once, the Athenian army made ready to march out against the enemy.

The army was made up of men who were ordinary citizens most of the time—bakers, merchants, craftsmen, and so on. But a Greek regarded it as a duty and an honor to fight for his city. These men owned their own armor and weapons, and trained steadily. They were skilled and brave soldiers.

There were no bowmen or horse soldiers in the Athenian army. All the men were foot soldiers. Each man wore a helmet and body and leg armor. And

each carried a sword, a long spear, and a large, round shield. The nine-foot (2.7-meter) spear, used for jabbing and stabbing, was the main weapon. Only if his spear were broken would a Greek draw his sword to hack at his enemies.

The helmet, made of bronze—a gold-colored metal that is a mixture of tin and copper—covered the whole head, the back of the neck, and most of the face. The inside was lined with leather or heavy cloth. Most helmets had big, curved crests of thick, colored horsehair. Such a crest looked like a decoration, but it actually had an important purpose—it could keep a sword from cutting into a man's head.

Greek war helmets from the time of Marathon. The bottom one belonged to a soldier named Dendas.

Body armor was a sleeveless shirt of tough leather or linen cloth, with thin strips or scales of bronze sewn onto it. Flaps of leather protected the shoulders, and a kind of skirt of leather straps hung from the waist to protect the thighs. Leg armor was thin tubes of bronze, slit up the back, which slipped onto a man's legs from knee to ankle. But most soldiers were barefoot, for many Greeks went barefoot all the time, even in battle.

Greek soldiers were well protected with armor, helmets, and thick shields.

The shield was made of thick wood covered with a layer of tough bull hide or a sheet of bronze. Many shields were painted with designs, such as the figure of an owl, a symbol of Athena (uh THEE nuh), the goddess of Athens.

Thus, a Greek soldier's armor protected him from cuts and stabs, and his shield protected him from spear thrusts. All this armor and equipment was actually quite light. A fully equipped Greek soldier could move easily, fight well, and even run at nearly top speed.

The Athenian soldiers, about nine

thousand strong, assembled in the market place. There, they and all the other citizens, looking up into the sky, prayed for victory. Then the soldiers marched off through the narrow, stony streets and out the huge gate. No band played for the Athenian army as it marched away to battle. But all the citizens came to see their men leave, and watched until they were out of sight.

When the Athenian army reached the hills above the plain of Marathon, it

This arrowhead was found on the plain of Marathon and was probably used in the battle.

halted and made camp. Suddenly, someone saw another Greek army marching through the hills toward them. It was the army of the tiny city of Plataea, only some one thousand strong. But these brave men had come to help the Athenians.

It was then that the eleven Athenian and Plataean commanders walked to the crest of the hill to study their enemy. The soldiers of the Persian Empire looked nothing at all like the Greeks. They came from many parts of the empire, and wore different kinds of clothing. There were Persians in colorful, big-sleeved, ankle-length robes, and Medes in knee-length jackets, baggy pants, and short boots, as well as men of many other lands. Their weapons were short spears, swords, axes, and bows and arrows. Few had any armor.

The Greek commanders began to talk over what they should do. The Persians vastly outnumbered the Greek army—and

this wasn't even the whole Persian force. The other half of the Persian army was still encamped near Eretria. It was actually that part of the Persian force that had some of the Athenian commanders most worried. What if it should attack Athens while the Athenian army was at Marathon?

This was why one of the Greek leaders, a sharp-nosed, curly bearded man whose name was Miltiades (mihl TY uh deez), wanted to attack the Persians at once. "The longer we wait, the greater the danger to Athens," he argued. "We must

Soldiers of the Persian Empire came from many parts of the Near East. Most of them had no armor such as the Greeks wore.

push these Persians into the sea and return to Athens at once!"

"Miltiades is right," said a commander named Aristides (ar ihs TY deez). "We cannot afford to wait."

But one of the other commanders pointed toward the Persians. "Those men have conquered half the world, and they outnumber us two to one!" he exclaimed. "They have thousands of bowmen, while we have none. They have hundreds of horsemen, and we have none. How do we dare attack?"

"I tell you, we can beat them!" insisted Miltiades. "I have fought against them in the Near East, and I have seen their weaknesses. Most of them are just *slave* soldiers—men from lands the Persians have conquered. They have no real wish to fight for the Persian emperor. Why, their commanders *force* them into battle by lashing them with whips! Their weapons are poor compared to ours, and they have no armor. They may outnumber us, but they will not fight as hard as we, who will be fighting for our land, our homes, and our loved ones. Each Greek will be worth two or three of such men!"

They thought over what he had said. Then, another man spoke.

"What you say may be true, Miltiades. Perhaps we can beat them. But we must *reach* them first. All those bowmen can rain thousands of arrows down on us while we are marching toward them. We will die by the hundreds before we ever reach the Persian line."

Miltiades grinned at him, dark eyes shining with confidence. "I know how we can prevent that! We will march toward the Persians until we get into range of their arrows—then we run the rest of the

This is an ancient stone sculpture of the head of Miltiades.

way! We will be upon them before they have time to shoot many arrows."

This seemed a daring plan, for Greek armies always marched slowly in a huge, tight crowd against their foes. But some of the commanders began to nod their heads in agreement.

"It is a good plan, Miltiades," said the commander named Aristides.

Miltiades glanced around at the faces of the others. Perhaps he had convinced most of them. "Let us put it to a vote," he suggested. "I vote we attack *now*!"

There were five votes for, and five against—a tie! Miltiades took a deep breath and turned to the man who had not yet voted. This was Callimachus (kah LIHM uh kuhs), the high commander.

"It is up to you, Callimachus," Miltiades told him. "Your vote can either enslave Athens or keep her free. For I tell you, if we do not attack—if we wait—the city may be taken by that other Persian army!" He reached out and put his hand on the high commander's shoulder. "But if we attack now, we will *win* and keep Athens free!"

Callimachus looked thoughtfully at him for a few moments without saying anything. Then he nodded. "I vote with you, Miltiades. We shall attack."

The commanders turned and made their way back to the waiting army. Miltiades gave a short speech, explaining what he wanted the men to do. Then, Callimachus gave the command to advance. With the clank and rustle of armor and the rumble of ten thousand pairs of feet, the men of Greece moved down the hillside. The sunlight gleaming on their bronze helmets, armor, and shields made them look like an army clad in gold. Partway down the hill, someone began to chant a battle hymn. At once, the entire army joined in. The valley rang with the sound of ten thousand voices.

Among the soldiers of the Persian Empire, busy with many tasks in their

camp on the beach, shouts of surprise
sounded. For a moment, they stared at
the golden line moving down the hillside.
Then their commanders lashed out with
their whips and shouted for the men to
form a line of battle. Drums began to
boom and horns began to blare the
alarm. Spearmen snatched up their
weapons and shields and rushed to form
ranks. Bowmen hurriedly strung their
bows.

When the Greek army reached the
plain of Marathon, Miltiades arranged
the soldiers in a long line that stretched
across the entire width of the plain. The
middle of the line was only about four

This picture from an ancient Greek drinking cup shows a fight between a Greek and a Persian. Perhaps the artist fought for freedom at Marathon.

men deep, but each end of the line was about eight men deep.

Moving rapidly, the Greeks soon drew close to the Persians. Miltiades judged the distance carefully. Just before the Greeks got close enough for Persian arrows to reach them—about 200 yards (180 m) —he gave a signal. A trumpet screamed. As they had been told to do when they heard that sound, the Greek soldiers instantly broke into a dead run. Feet kicking up brown spurts of dust, they came racing at the Persians!

As Miltiades had predicted, archers had time to shoot only one or two poorly aimed arrows before the Greek army smashed into the Persian line. The plain of Marathon erupted with the sounds of battle— shouts, the stamping of feet, the thud of weapons striking shields. Men stood face to face, stabbing at each other with spears, each using his shield to block the other man's thrust.

The middle part of the Persian line was formed mainly of Medes and Persians. These were some of the empire's best soldiers. They were well armed and well equipped. Matched against the thinnest part of the Greek line, they vastly outnumbered the enemy. Slowly but surely they forced the Greek center to give ground.

But on the sides, or "wings" of both battle lines, things were very different. The wings of the Persian army were made up of Bactrians, Lydians, and men from other lands that Persia had conquered. Again, Miltiades had been right, for these men were no match for the soldiers of Greece. Their short, light spears bounced off the tough Greek shields, and glanced off bronze helmets and body armor. But the stout spears of the Greeks tore right through the flimsy, wicker Persian shields and ripped into bodies covered only by thin clothing. On both wings, the Greeks pushed in and the enemy began to draw back.

Thus, while the center of the Persian battle line was pushing forward, the two

wings were moving back and *in*. What
had been a long, straight line now
became U-shaped! The Greek line
suddenly became a clamp, squeezing the
Persians together from two sides.
Thousands of Persians, caught in a
struggling crowd in the middle, were
unable to get to the fighting. Even though
the Greeks were outnumbered, most of
the Persian soldiers couldn't get at them.

And on the wings, the Greeks were
doing terrible damage to their enemies.
The soldiers of the Persian Empire were
falling by the score to the stabbing spears
of the Greeks. Suddenly, panic erupted
among the Persians! Trickles of men
began to slip off to the side, away from
the battle. The trickles became streams,
and the streams became a flood.
Abruptly, the entire Persian army
dissolved into a mob of running men.
Yelling in fear, they pushed and shoved
each other in their effort to get away!

The Persians fled through their camp,
pursued by the triumphantly yelling
Greeks who cut them down by the dozen
as they ran, or seized them by their robes,
making them captives. The Persians

gathered on the beach, some straining to push their ships into the water, others striving to hold back the Greeks. As the ships slid into the water, Persians scrambled aboard and began trying to row to safety. Greeks swarmed into the water, trying to seize the ships and keep them from getting away. Enough Greeks managed to climb onto seven ships to capture them, but the rest escaped out to sea.

The Battle of Marathon was over, and it
was an amazing victory for the Greeks.
More than six thousand soldiers of Persia
had been killed, wounded, or captured,
but fewer than two hundred Greeks had
fallen! Miltiades had been right. Their
armor had protected them and they had
fought harder because of their love of
freedom. His faith in them, and their
courage against almost overwhelming
odds, had won the marvelous victory.

But things were not quite over, yet.
Miltiades feared that the Persian fleet
would sail around the southern end of
Greece and attack Athens from the sea.
So he led the victorious army back
through the hills to the city. The men
marched all night and before sunrise
they reached the hills overlooking the
coast just beyond Athens.

Sure enough, as the sun rose, the ships
of the Persian fleet could be seen, moving
toward the land. But at the sight of the
Athenian army standing on the hillside,
the ships turned and headed back out to
sea. Now, the battle for freedom was
truly over. The invasion had been defeated.
Athens, and all of Greece, were still free!

The battle in the forest

The Battle of the
Teutoburg Forest
Germany, A.D. 9

The army moved slowly through the great Teutoburg (TOY toh burk) forest that spread out in all directions. Thousands of big, shaggy, gray-trunked oak trees grew close together. Their leafy branches twined and crisscrossed overhead, forming a roof of leaves. The forest was dim and gloomy, for very little light came through this thick greenery.

The soldiers, small, sturdy, dark-eyed and dark-haired men, wore iron helmets and armor that covered the upper part of the body. Their legs were bare, but they had leather sandals on their feet.

the city of Rome

Each man carried a spear with a long, thin, iron point, and a big rectangular shield. The shields were made of wood covered with colored leather, and each had a metal decoration. A short sword hung at each man's right side.

These were soldiers of the mighty Roman Empire in the year we call A.D. 9 —nearly two thousand years ago. At that time, the city of Rome ruled all of Italy. Its armies had also conquered Greece, parts of the Near East, much of western Europe, and Britain. Now, Rome was trying to conquer the land of Germany. A Roman army had invaded the country, and ships of the Roman navy sailed on

a German village

German rivers. Forts had been built, from which Roman commanders ruled the countryside.

This part of Germany was a land of thick forests and broad swamps. It was mostly a wilderness, with no cities or roads. But it was home to a number of tribes who lived in small villages, usually in a clearing beside a river. The people made their living by hunting and farming.

When the Romans invaded their country, the Germans tried to fight back. Although they were strong and brave, they had no armor and their main weapons were just poorly made spears. Their way of fighting was to rush at an

Roman soldiers were well trained in the use of their weapons.

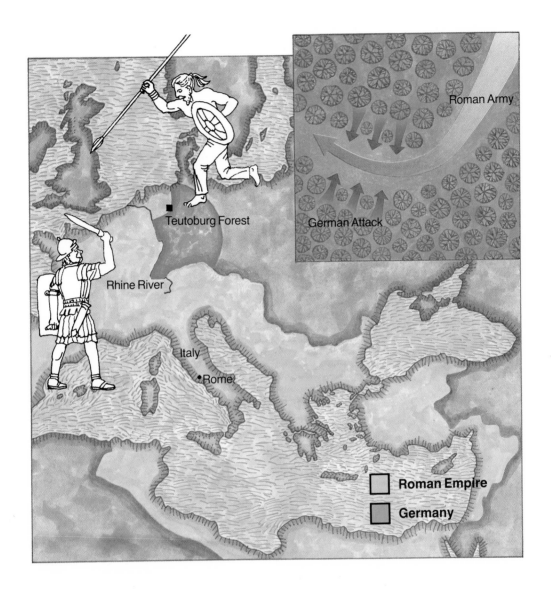

Teutoburg Forest

Rhine River

Italy

•Rome

Roman Army

German Attack

☐ **Roman Empire**

☐ **Germany**

enemy, stabbing and thrusting with their
spears. But this did not work against the
Romans. The Romans were skillful
soldiers, well equipped and well trained.
And they were led by smart, experienced
commanders. They had a way of fighting
that won most of their battles.

A Roman fighting force, called a legion, had about five thousand men, divided into ten groups. In battle formation, each group was fifty men wide and ten men deep. These groups formed up in three

lines, four groups in the first line and
three groups each in the second and third
lines.

When the enemy charged, the Romans
waited until they were about twenty
yards (18 meters) away. Then, two ranks
at a time, the men in the first line hurled
their spears. Many enemy warriors,
struck by spears, went down. Others
tripped over fallen men. Some simply
stopped, shocked and stunned by the
sight of their fallen comrades. All four
groups in the first line then drew their

swords and charged. Often, this was enough to make the enemy turn and run!

In this way, the Romans had beaten the Germans and become their rulers. A proud, warlike people, most Germans were overcome with rage and shame at having lost their freedom.

But some Germans became friendly with the Romans. Next to the Roman commander of the army moving through the forest rode a young, well-dressed German. A prince of one of the German tribes, his name was Hermann (HUR mahn). But the Romans called him Arminius (ahr MIHN ee uhs).

When the Romans found that Arminius seemed friendly, they had done all they could to

Shown above are the remains of an actual Roman sword and scabbard, and a model of what these looked like when they were in use.

encourage his friendship. They had taken him to Rome, where he was entertained, honored, and given gifts. Thus, Arminius had come to know the Romans well, and the Romans felt he had been won over to their side. They helped him organize a force of several thousand of his tribe's warriors to help the Roman soldiers keep peace in Germany.

Then news came that some German villages had risen in revolt against the Romans. Arminius and his men went with three Roman legions sent to end the uprising. As the army tramped through the forest, Arminius often rode with the commander, General Varus (VAIR uhs) and other Roman officers.

Behind them, the army was strung out in a long line that stretched for miles (kilometers). There were some fifteen thousand Roman troops and about five

thousand Germans under Arminius.
Many of the soldiers had their families
with them, so that there were perhaps
ten thousand other people. There were
also some fifteen hundred pack mules
and many horse-drawn wagons carrying
tents, food, and other supplies.

It had been raining steadily for several
days. Water poured down from the trees,
making the ground underfoot slick with
mud and wet leaves.

"Does it always rain like this in your
country, Arminius?" asked one of the

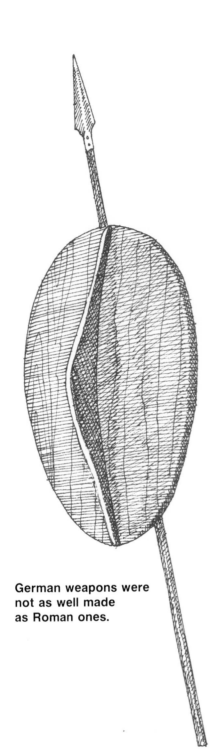

German weapons were
not as well made
as Roman ones.

Romans, shivering in a soaking-wet cloak. "I've never seen such gloom!"

"Things will get better soon," Arminius promised with a smile.

Suddenly there were shouts from behind. Arminius and the others turned to see what was happening. A soldier on horseback came riding as fast as he could up the narrow trail that wound through the trees. Foot soldiers scrambled to get out of his way.

"General Varus," shouted the horseman. "We are being attacked!"

"What?" exclaimed Varus. "Where?"

The man pulled up his horse beside the general. "Small bands of Germans have attacked us at several places along the line of march, General," he told Varus. "They came rushing out of the trees, killed a number of our soldiers, and disappeared back into the woods. They always picked a thin place in the line, where they outnumbered our men. They've taken some of our pack mules, too!"

Varus frowned. "They can't do any real damage to us with such tricks. But they'll keep the men on edge wondering where they're going to strike next."

"I had better get back to my men," said Arminius. He turned his horse around and started back down the trail.

After a time, Arminius reached the part of the line formed by his German soldiers. He slipped down off his horse and, leading it along, began to walk among the men.

"Small bands of our countrymen are attacking the Romans," said Arminius. "You know what we must do now."

The men nodded. Some of them dropped back to talk with others. Soon, little groups of German warriors began to slip off into the woods. Before long, everyone had disappeared. Later, when a messenger from Varus came looking for Arminius, he could not find anyone.

Arminius led his horse into the forest. He walked through the woods until he came to where thousands of German

warriors stood, sat, and crouched among
the trees. These were Arminius' men and
many others as well.

They looked nothing at all like the
Roman soldiers. Few of the Germans had
a helmet of any kind, and none had
armor. Most of the men were bareheaded,
bare chested, and barefoot, clad only in
trousers made of leather. Some had a
long-sleeved, shirtlike jacket of leather or
wool, and a few had cloaks of animal fur.

Most had only a spear and an oval shield
made of wood. A few had long swords
as well.

Nearly all had beards and long hair.
Many of the younger men had let their
hair grow until it hung down over their
faces. They had sworn not to cut their hair
or show their faces until they had wiped
out the shame of the Roman conquest.

Arminius walked slowly among these
men, talking so that all could hear.

"We will keep attacking in small groups for a time, to weaken the Romans and frighten them," he said. "Then, when I give the signal, we shall all attack at once! We will wipe out these Roman pigs who think they have conquered our land! We will make Germany free again!"

Arminius was not a friend of Rome after all. He had tricked the Romans into thinking so, and now had set a trap for them. Arminius had caused the uprisings that had made the Romans send their army into the forest, where the soldiers would be spread out in a long line. He had secretly arranged for thousands of German warriors to meet in the forest. And he had planned the attacks that he hoped would destroy the Roman army.

As Arminius had told them to do, the Germans kept making small attacks all along the stretched-out line of Roman soldiers. A cluster of Romans, slogging along beneath the dripping trees, would suddenly have a shower of spears come whizzing out of the forest at them. Another group, at another part of the line, would find a swarm of yelling German warriors charging them.

Varus, the Roman commander, knew his army was in trouble. It was much weaker now that Arminius and his German warriors were gone. The constant attacks made the soldiers nervous and fearful. Spread out as they were, and surrounded by trees, they could not get into battle formation.

Arminius decided that the time had come for the main attack. Lifting a horn to his lips, Arminius blew a long, loud note. The sound carried through the forest and was heard by both Germans and Romans.

At once, the forest exploded with the roar of thousands of voices as all the

Germans charged, each man yelling at the top of his lungs. All along the Roman line, German warriors burst out of the trees and rushed at their foes.

The Romans were brave, and most of them had been in battle before. They had helmets and armor, better shields, and better weapons than the Germans. But most of the Germans were much bigger than the Romans, and they were all wild with anger at these invaders. They were willing to die in order to drive the Romans out!

The Germans' size and their fierce anger might have made little difference had the Romans been in battle formation. But in a fight of man against man, these things made a big difference.

For several days, the Germans and Romans engaged in a bloody, running struggle. Finally, the Germans overwhelmed the legions and destroyed them. Of the fifteen thousand Roman soldiers General Varus had led into the Teutoburg Forest, only a few managed to escape. Badly wounded, and shamed by the crushing defeat, General Varus killed himself.

A monument with a huge statue of Arminius now stands in the forest in West Germany near where the battle took place.

To the Romans, Arminius was a traitor. But to his own people, Arminius was a hero. He knew that the Germans could not defeat a Roman army that was in battle formation. So, he tricked General Varus into leading his army into a forest where they would have to fight man to man.

This defeat was one of the worst the Roman Empire ever suffered. So many soldiers were lost that the Romans did not dare stay in Germany. They pulled back across the Rhine River, and Germany was free again.

Turning back the tide

The Battle of Tours
France, A.D. 732

A stream of people moved along a narrow dirt road that ran through the countryside in western France. Most of them carried bundles of food and belongings. One little girl pulled a goat along by a piece of rope around its neck. A boy carried a small pig in his arms. All these people had worried, frightened faces. They often turned their heads to glance fearfully back up the road. Somewhere behind them, they knew, death was approaching!

It was the year 732, more than twelve hundred years ago, and terror hung over western France. An army had invaded the land, burning and

destroying villages, towns, and cities. And it was slaughtering or enslaving every man, woman, and child in its path. People were leaving their farms and homes to hide in forests and caves, or were fleeing eastward with as many of their belongings as they could carry.

To the people of France, who called themselves Franks, the invading army was an army of demons that spread darkness and evil across the land! The Franks were Christians, but the invaders were fierce enemies of Christianity—Arabs, Moors, and Berbers from Arabia and North Africa. They were Muslims (MUHZ luhmz) and followed the religion of Islam (IHS luhm). They intended to

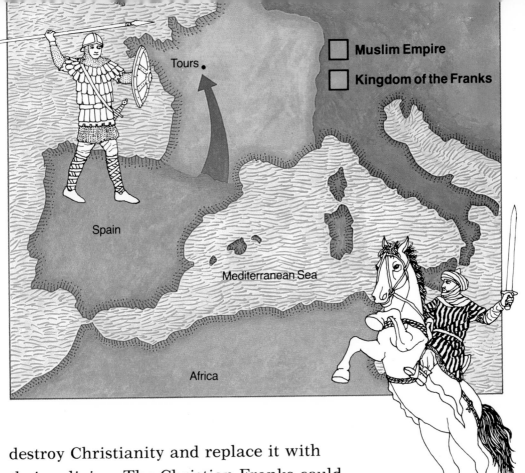

Muslim Empire

Kingdom of the Franks

Spain

Mediterranean Sea

Africa

destroy Christianity and replace it with
their religion. The Christian Franks could
not imagine anything more dreadful.

It seemed as if nothing could stop the
Muslims. They had conquered North
Africa, much of the Near East, and most
of Spain. Now this Muslim army had
come over the mountains from Spain and
was halfway into France. An army of
Franks, led by Eudo (oo doh), Duke of
Aquitaine (AK wih tayn), had tried to stop
the invaders but had been wiped out. It
looked as if the Muslims might go on
through France and conquer all of Europe!

The Franks had only one hope left. The
ruler of the northern part of France,

whose name was Charles, was leading an army westward to fight the Muslims. Charles was forty-four years old and had been fighting most of his life. A famous warrior, he had won many battles against the people of Holland and Germany, who often raided Frankish lands.

Charles led his army through hills, trying to keep hidden. He hoped to get close to the Muslims before they found out he was coming. He knew full well they were the most dangerous enemy he had ever faced.

But the Muslim commander, Abd-er-Rahman (uhb dur ra MAHN), was also a skilled warrior. He had groups of men on fast horses out scouting the

countryside. Some of these scouts soon
found Charles's army.

The Muslim invaders were camped
outside the city of Tours (toor).
Abd-er-Rahman intended to plunder and
burn Tours as he had other Frankish
cities his army had taken. As he sat in
his tent, a soldier entered and bowed. "Oh
Commander of the Faithful, an army of
Franks has been seen moving toward us,"
the man reported.

Abd-er-Rahman stroked his beard and
thought about what he should do. He, too,

had spent most of his life fighting. He did not fear going into battle against Charles's army. However, the Muslims had collected an enormous amount of treasure from all the towns and cities they had taken. This treasure greatly concerned Abd-er-Rahman. He could not take it into battle. Nor could he leave it behind in the camp. If he did, the people of Tours might try to recapture it while the Muslim army was away.

Abd-er-Rahman finally decided to send the treasure back to Spain. He would move his army with it part of the way, until he was sure it would be safe. Then, he would turn back and destroy this Frankish army that was looking for him!

For a week, the Muslim army moved back in the direction it had come from. Charles and his men followed, cautiously. Then, some of his scouts came riding to tell him that the Muslims were no longer on the move. They had stopped and were making ready for battle. Abd-er-Rahman had decided that the treasure, carried by scores of mules, could be sent on under the guard of just a few men. Now, he intended to attack the Franks!

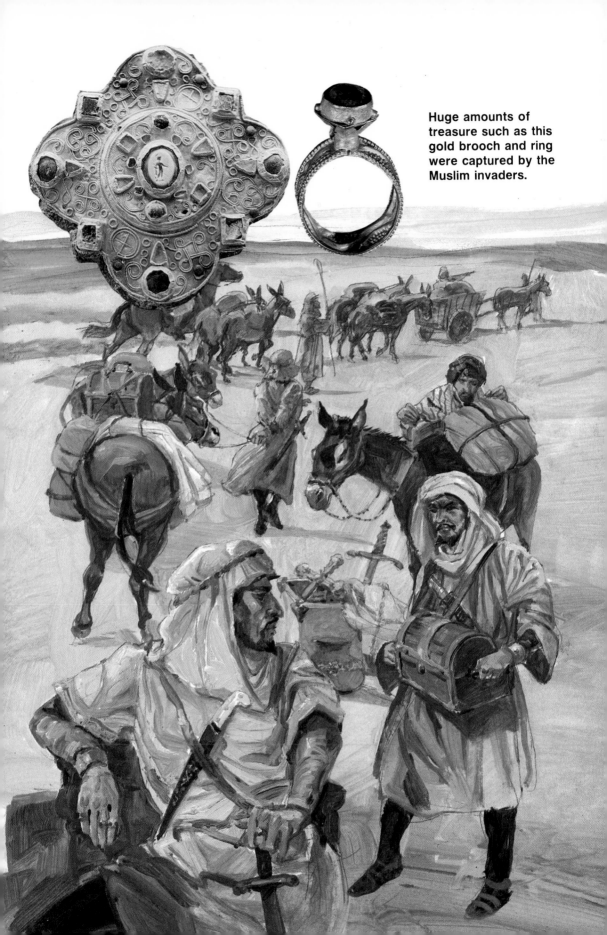

Huge amounts of treasure such as this gold brooch and ring were captured by the Muslim invaders.

The Muslims were all horsemen. Most of them wore only light robes and turbans, and carried only a long lance or a straight, sharp-edged sword. Their small, swift horses could carry them easily and move fast. The Muslim way of fighting was to make a wild, headlong charge, smashing into their enemies and scattering them.

The Frankish army was very different. Most of Charles's men were foot soldiers, and many of them were heavily armored. They wore bowl-shaped helmets of iron and leather coats on which rows of iron scales were sewn. Their weapons were a sturdy spear and a sword or ax. And they carried

a Frankish soldier

round shields made of wood strengthened with strips of iron. Their way of fighting, too, was to charge at their enemy.

But Charles knew that foot soldiers could not charge men on horses. He had another plan, and he quickly called his commanders together to explain it.

"I shall form the army into one great, solid square," he told them. "We shall simply stand and let the enemy charge us. We will make them waste their strength trying to break into our square, like ocean waves trying to smash open a great, solid rock!"

The Frankish commanders went among the men to explain the plan. The few horse soldiers in the Frankish army got off their horses to stand with the others. Soon, the army had formed a huge square, as Charles wanted. The men stood shoulder to shoulder, row upon row, their dragon banners fluttering in the breeze.

Every Frankish soldier knew that the future of his land depended upon this battle. If the Muslims won, they would conquer the land of the Franks. They would burn and rob and destroy, for there would be no one to stop them. Every Frank not killed would be made a slave.

Abd-er-Rahman led his army toward the Franks. He did not think it would matter that they were packed into such a thick formation. His wild, fierce warriors were more than willing to die for their religion. He felt they would smash into the Frankish force and break it apart, as they had done so many times with other armies.

His sword hissed as he slid it from its scabbard. Waving it in the air, he

Frankish banners were tubes of leather or cloth painted to look like a dragon. The wind made them wiggle and flutter.

shouted, "God is with us! In the name of the Faith, attack!"

With wild yells, the desert warriors thundered toward the Frankish square. They expected the force of their charge to shatter the formation—but that didn't happen. With their shields raised and spears and axes at the ready, the Franks stood like a wall. Stabbing with their spears and slashing with their swords, the Muslims tried to force their way into the square. But the Franks stood firm. When a Frankish soldier fell, another quickly moved forward to take his place. Protecting themselves with their sturdy shields, the Franks stabbed and hacked back at the milling horsemen.

a Frankish war ax

After a time, the Muslims realized they were not making any headway. At first a few, and then by the hundreds, they retreated.

"Once again, my brothers," called Abd-er-Rahman. "We shall break them open and scatter them to the winds! In God's name, follow me!"

83

Again, the Muslim horsemen came charging in a great wave at the Frankish square. But this charge, too, failed to break the square.

Again and again, throughout the long afternoon, the Muslims charged the square. A great cloud of dust, kicked up by the galloping hoofs of the horses, hung over the battlefield. A huge pile of dead and wounded Muslims and Franks, as well as horses, lay before the square. The sturdy Franks stood shoulder to shoulder, grimly gripping their weapons. Charles moved among them, talking to keep up their spirits.

"Hold on, men," he urged. "They cannot keep coming at us much longer. We are wearing them down. They cannot break us, and they will have to give up. We will show them they cannot conquer us!"

What he said was true. The unarmored Muslims had lost far more men than the Franks, who were protected by their armor and shields. The Muslim charges were getting weaker. Surprised that they hadn't been able to break into the square, the Muslims began to grow worried.

Then, near sunset, as Abd-er-Rahman led still another charge, an ax thrown by a Frankish soldier struck him on the head. He slid from his horse and lay motionless on the ground.

"The commander has been slain!" yelled a Muslim warrior who had seen what happened. Word quickly spread through the Muslim army. Now the horsemen wheeled their steeds about and rode away from the deadly square of Frankish soldiers. The loss of their leader had taken the heart for battle out of them.

"They are beaten!" cried Charles. "They may try again, but they are beaten! We have won!"

He was right. The Frankish soldiers stayed in place, ready to fight off another attack. But as twilight darkened into night, no attack came. When the sky lightened in the morning, the Franks peered out at the plain and saw that the Muslims had gone! Under cover of darkness, the invaders had stolen away, back toward Spain. They had lost a great many men and had seen that they could not defeat a Frankish force that held its ground.

The victory at Tours ended the Muslim

threat to the land of the Franks and to all
of Europe. After this great battle, Charles
was called Charles Martel (mahr TEHL),
meaning "the Hammer," and became
ruler of all the Franks.

For many more years, Franks and
Muslims warred against each other with
quick raids and border battles. But never
again did the Muslims attempt to conquer
this Christian kingdom. Charles Martel
and his square of sturdy iron-armored
Franks had kept their land free.

Warriors of the Rising Sun

The Mongol invasion
Japan, 1281

It was a bright, warm morning in June. White clouds drifted through the blue sky, and the songs of birds filled the air.

But Mosuke Ogasawara (MOH soo kay oh gah sah wah rah) had no time to enjoy the beauty of the day. He was putting on his battle armor. Mosuke was a Japanese warrior—a samurai (SAM u ry). Soon he would be fighting the Hairy Barbarians who were coming to try to conquer Japan!

Around his legs, Mosuke tied shin guards of leather. Thigh guards of varnished iron scales, tied together with brightly colored cords of silk, went around his waist. They hung down to his knees. On each

arm he tied an arm guard of varnished metal.

Then, Mosuke put on a sleeveless cloth coat. Sewn onto it in rows were strips of iron and of colored leather. Over his shoulders he fastened shoulder guards of leather and iron. Then he tied a strip of silk cloth around his head, to hold his long black hair in place. Finally, he placed his iron helmet on his head. Now, with his two swords fastened at his waist, his quiver of arrows hanging from his right side, and his long bow in his hand, Mosuke Ogasawara, warrior of the Land of the Rising Sun, was ready for battle.

For seven years, the people of the Land of the Rising Sun had been awaiting an invasion of their country. Now, the invasion had begun. Across the Yellow Sea from China had come thousands of ships,

samurai armor

bringing many thousands of soldiers of the Mongol (MAHN guhl) Empire—the Hairy Barbarians. And another Mongol fleet had arrived from nearby Korea. Today, the enemy would try to fight their way ashore, to begin the conquest of the land.

Seven years earlier, the Mongols had tried to conquer the Land of the Rising Sun. In the year 1274, a Mongol army had landed in the southern part of the country, on the island of Kyushu (KYOO shoo). Quickly, the warlords who ruled Kyushu had formed an army and attacked the invaders, trying to push them back into the sea. But the Japanese warriors had been badly defeated.

However, the invasion failed when a terrible storm began to rage. Many of the Mongol ships sank. Fearing that all the ships might sink if they remained anchored, the Mongol commanders brought their soldiers back onto the remaining ships and sailed away.

But Mosuke Ogasawara and every other Japanese knew that the Mongols would return. The Mongol emperor, Kublai Khan (KOO bluh kahn), had sent

This old painting shows samurai warriors defending the long stone wall on the coast of Kyushu.

messengers demanding that Japan surrender and become part of the Mongol Empire. Angrily, the Japanese ruler, the Shogun (SHOH guhn), or commanding general, Tokimune (toh kee moo nay), had the messengers beheaded! Everyone knew that Kublai Khan would want revenge for that. The Mongols would come again, to punish the Land of the Rising Sun!

At once, the people of Japan began to get ready for the return of their enemies. On Kyushu, they built a long stone wall all along the part of the coast where the Mongols had landed before. Tokimune sent ships and warriors to Kyushu, and had weapons manufactured and stored away. Each day, the soldiers and sailors trained.

Then, after seven years had passed, Japanese spies sent word that two great

Mongol fleets had set sail and were
heading for the Land of the Rising Sun.

   The Japanese people knew they faced a
terrible struggle. The Mongol Empire was
the most enormous empire that had ever
existed anywhere in the world. It covered
what is now China, North and South
Korea, southern Russia, Afghanistan,

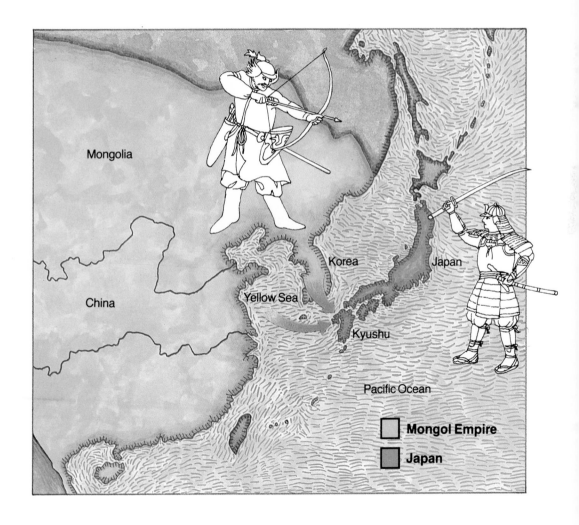

Iran, Iraq, Mongolia, and parts of Europe and Southeast Asia. It could send an army of a hundred thousand men against its enemies—and the army of the Mongol Empire had never been defeated!

The Mongol army consisted mostly of horsemen who were skilled archers. These men fought in groups and were trained to obey instantly the commands of their leaders. The Mongols also possessed "secret weapons," such as a catapult (a kind of giant slingshot) that hurled burning and exploding missiles.

a samurai sword

The Japanese army that would face the Mongols was very different. It was formed mostly of foot soldiers who carried spears with long, curved points, and of samurai warriors such as Mosuke Ogasawara. Although the samurai were also horsemen and skillful archers, they did not fight in groups, as the Mongols did. Each samurai fought for himself, picking out one enemy warrior and challenging him to combat.

The foot soldiers were commoners. But the samurai were noblemen, whose fathers had been samurai and whose sons would be samurai also. The word *samurai* means "one who serves," and most samurai served as soldiers for great noblemen called daimyo (DY myoh). For a samurai, being true to the man he served, and being brave in battle, were the most important things in life.

Mosuke Ogasawara's commander had ordered him, along with many other samurai and common soldiers, to stand behind the long stone wall that stretched along part of the coast of Kyushu. Here, they would be protected from arrows

until the time came to rush at the enemy. Other groups of samurai, on horseback, waited at the end of the wall, and many samurai and foot soldiers were aboard the small, fast boats that would attack the ships of the Mongols.

Beside Mosuke stood his friend, another samurai named Katsutoyo (kat soo TOY oh).

The Mongol invaders begin their attack.

The armor of Japanese samurai warriors
was made of strips of iron and leather.

Looking out over the water, they could see the approaching Mongol ships stretching across the distant horizon.

"They are as many as the stars in the sky," said Katsutoyo, calmly.

Mosuke nodded. The warriors of the Land of the Rising Sun would be terribly outnumbered by the Mongols. Mosuke felt sure he would be killed fighting the invaders. But this did not frighten him, for every samurai expected to die in battle. For a samurai, life was like the life of a cherry blossom in the spring—beautiful, but very short.

By noon, the first of the ships were anchored off the shore and Mongol soldiers were swarming onto the beach. They wore long coats that hung to their knees, boots with pointed toes, and metal helmets. They carried long swords, spears, and curved bows. They began to shoot arrows at the men of Japan behind the stone wall.

As was the battle custom in the Land of the Rising Sun, Japanese warriors pounded gongs and bells. Archers shot arrows back at the Mongols.

Shouting, the Mongol soldiers charged

toward the wall. A row of samurai
warriors with their long, two-handed
swords awaited them.

Mosuke was in the front row of the
warriors of the Rising Sun. He did not
like the way he had to fight these
barbarians. He could not choose an
opponent and call out a challenge to him
as Japanese warriors did when they
fought each other. He had to fight anyone
who came at him. He had to cut down as
many of the enemy as he could, before

they killed or wounded him. He used his sword in a zigzag style of fighting, so that the movement of the blade formed a glittering pattern in front of him.

The fight went on for a long time, then the Mongol soldiers began to draw back. They could not get past the stone wall.

By the next day, more Mongol ships and more

soldiers had arrived. But they did not attack the wall at the place where Mosuke and the others waited. Instead, they attacked farther down the coast, trying to get around the wall. However, there they ran into samurai on horseback, who charged into them, shooting arrows and using their long swords. The Mongols were driven back to their ships.

On the next day, the Mongols attacked another part of the wall. But the samurai and other Japanese soldiers there held them back. Fighting also went on among the ships. The small, fast, Japanese boats, filled with warriors, attacked the Mongol ships. Several of the ships were set afire and sank.

Day after day, the battle continued. Many times Mosuke stood at the wall, using his sword as the Mongols tried to push through the Japanese force. At other times, he and the other warriors charged the Mongols, pushing them into the sea so that they had to return to their ships.

Once, Mosuke was slightly wounded by a gash on the cheek, but he kept on fighting. After one battle, he could not

find his friend, Katsutoyo. Later, he
learned that Katsutoyo had been killed.
Mosuke was happy for him, for he had
died with honor, fighting as a samurai
should.

Weeks passed, then a whole month.
Still the Mongols were unable to break
past the wall. But Mongol ships still

The temple of Ise, as it looks today. This is where the Japanese prayed to their sun goddess for help against the Mongols.

arrived, bringing more and more soldiers, while the Japanese force grew ever smaller. Soon, the Japanese would be so badly outnumbered they would not be able to hold back the Mongols no matter how well they fought.

By the fifty-third day, Mosuke knew it was hopeless. There were too many Mongols. In the next day or so, they would make a tremendous attack that would finally wipe out the warriors of the Rising Sun.

"We cannot save the land," Mosuke sadly told another samurai named Shigenari (shee gehn AHR ee). "They will overwhelm us. We can only die fighting, honorably."

"There is one hope," said Shigenari. "A special messenger has been sent to the great holy place at Ise (EE sah), to pray to the Sun Goddess, asking that the invaders be destroyed."

Mosuke bowed his head, respectfully. Will the goddess grant such a prayer, he wondered.

Near evening, the sky began to fill with dark clouds, and a strong wind began to blow. It grew stronger during the night, and by morning it blew with a raging fury that sent huge waves rushing across the sea. It was the kind of storm that is now known as a typhoon—a terrible windstorm like a hurricane.

The Mongol ships rocked and tossed in the water. Wave after wave smashed into them. As the waves grew ever higher, many of the ships began to fill with water and sink!

The Mongol commanders gave up all thought of trying to conquer Japan. Now, their only thought was to save as much of

their fleet as they could. As scores of ships sank, others pulled up anchor and tried to get out to sea. The Mongol soldiers on shore watched in despair as they saw the ships disappear. Without those ships, they were trapped in the land they had come to conquer.

With rain beating into their faces, Mosuke, Shigenari, and all the Japanese warriors watched with joy as the Mongol fleet was swept away. The invasion was over—Japan was still free!

"The Goddess has answered the prayer!" shouted Shigenari. "She has sent this great wind to destroy the invaders!"

To this day, the great typhoon that destroyed the Mongol fleet is spoken of in Japan as the *kamikaze* (kah mee KAH zee), or "divine wind." After the loss of his second fleet, the Mongol emperor, Kublai Khan, gave up trying to conquer Japan.

But it was not the divine wind alone that stopped the invasion. It was the courage and fighting ability of the Japanese samurai and other warriors. Although vastly outnumbered, they held the Mongols back for fifty-three days, until the storm struck.

The courage of the Mountai

The Battle of Sempach
Switzerland, July 9, 1386

The ground rumbled with
the tramp of sixteen hundred
marching men. The long line
moved slowly up a narrow
road that ran through a green
valley. In the distance, beyond
the surrounding fields, rose
towering mountains.

These were soldiers,
marching to war. Some carried
long-handled axes, called
halberds (HAL buhrds), and
others had big, heavy swords.
Most had long spears, called
pikes, three times longer than
a man. The pikes, held
straight up, looked like a
moving forest of thin tree
trunks.

The men wore jackets of
cloth or leather, and

The little cluster of cantons was partly surrounded by the large and powerful Holy Roman Empire. This empire covered most of what is now Austria, Germany, and part of Italy. Nearly a hundred years earlier, the cantons had been part of this empire and were ruled by its emperor. But they had broken away and declared themselves free. They had agreed to help each other, and, if necessary, stand together to fight for their freedom.

And they did have to fight. The emperor had sent an army to punish them and force them to rejoin the empire. But the Swiss soldiers had always managed to beat their enemies and keep the cantons free.

Now, Swiss soldiers were going to have to fight for freedom again. For, once more, the emperor had sent an army to punish the cantons. These marching Swiss soldiers were the advance guard of a Swiss army and were searching for the enemy.

The Swiss commander, riding on a horse some distance ahead of his troops tugged the reins to make the horse stop.

Leaning forward, he shaded his eyes and peered ahead. Then he whirled the horse about and came galloping back toward the marchers.

"Halt!" he shouted. "Form for battle! I can see them coming!"

Quickly, the Swiss soldiers formed a huge square made up of many rows of men. The square was just about as wide as it was deep. The men in the front row lowered their pikes. Then the men behind them lowered their pikes, holding them straight out over the shoulders of the men in front. The front of the square became a wall of sharp, gleaming points.

The Swiss knew that the enemy army was made up mostly of knights in armor, on horseback. Knights usually fought only one way—they galloped straight ahead in a charge, with their long lances held straight out. They would try to smash into the Swiss and scatter them.

But the Swiss had learned that the horses would not be able to get past the wall of pike points. The charge would come to a stop in front of the square, with knights and horses all jammed together, hardly able to move. Then those

a Swiss pikeman

Swiss armed with long swords and axes would rush out of the square to hack and chop at the helpless knights. This was how the Swiss had won their other battles.

Soon, the Swiss could see the enemy. The army of the empire was made up of three large groups of knights. There were a great many more of them than there were Swiss.

Even so, the soldiers of the Swiss advance guard felt sure they could handle these knights. And, if needed, their army was not far behind.

The commander of the emperor's army, Duke Leopold (LAY uh pohld) of Swabia, ordered his horsemen to halt. Lifting the visor of his helmet, he stared at the Swiss. It angered Leopold to think that men like these—common farmers and workmen—could have beaten an army of knights who, like Leopold, were all noblemen. He intended to punish them for that, as well as for daring to declare themselves free from the emperor's rule!

Leopold knew how the Swiss fought. He had spent a great deal of time thinking how to beat them. He was sure he had figured out the way. Today, he would put these commoners in their place. He would teach them a lesson they would never forget.

He rode to the leading group of knights,

two thousand strong. "The Swiss expect us to charge them and be slaughtered," he told them. "But we shall turn their own methods against them! Dismount, and form a square like theirs. Today, we shall fight as they do—on foot. We shall use our lances as they use their pikes. They cannot stand up to us, for they do not have armor as we do. And they are not our equals, for we are men of noble blood and they are mere peasants!"

The Swiss watched in surprise as one group of knights dismounted, formed a huge square, and began to move toward them with lances thrust out. They had not expected the Austrians to fight this way. The Swiss commander frowned in worry. He realized that the Austrians' armor would give them a big advantage.

The distance between the two squares got shorter. The Swiss in the front row gritted their teeth and gripped their pikes more tightly, knowing that they faced death or injury. The Austrians, sure their armor would protect them, strode steadily forward until the two walls of glittering points nearly touched.

Pikes and lances began to click together as the men in front dodged and thrust. Each square pushed at the other, trying

to force it backward or break it open. There was a steady rumble of stamping feet, and the air rang with yells, grunts, curses, and shrieks of pain. As men in the front fell to the ground, stabbed by enemy weapons, the men behind pushed forward to take their place.

Slowly but surely, the Swiss soldiers began to give ground. The Austrians' armor made a big difference. The points of the Swiss pikes often simply slid off the armor. But the Austrian lances sliced through the cloth and leather jackets of

115

the Swiss. The Swiss were losing more men than the Austrians. Their square began to weaken under the steady push of the Austrians.

The Swiss faced disaster. As the enemy's push grew stronger, the Swiss square would begin to crumble and break apart. This meant defeat! If the Austrians shattered the Swiss advance guard, their full army could strike without warning at the Swiss forces coming up from behind. With the Swiss army defeated, the Austrians would conquer the cantons and destroy the Swiss Confederation.

But now, according to tales of the battle that have come down to us through six hundred years, something heroic happened. It is said that a young Swiss soldier, Arnold von Winkelried (VIHNG kuhl reet) dropped his pike and spread his arms to gather in as many of the Austrian lance points as he could. Many of them pierced his body. But with so many lances pulled out of the way, an opening suddenly appeared in the front of the Austrian square.

At once, a Swiss soldier armed with a halberd rushed forward. With two mighty

This helmet is the kind worn by the Austrian knights at the Battle of Sempach.

swings he struck down two knights whose lances were held fast by the dying Winkelried. Their armor did not protect them against the tremendous blows of the sturdy mountaineer.

In moments, the axman was joined by a swordsman, swinging a long, heavy blade with both hands. As these men began to hack and carve their way into the Austrian square, more Swiss soldiers pushed in with them.

Everything suddenly changed! The slow, steady forward push of the Austrian knights halted. With Swiss axmen and swordsmen in among them, the knights were helpless. Their long lances were

useless at close range. The smashing blows of swords and halberd sliced right through their armor. As the knights saw those flashing swords and halberds move toward them, many simply dropped their lances and tried to push their way out of the square to safety!

Watching in horror, Duke Leopold saw the Austrian square begin to break apart. He turned his horse and galloped back to the other two groups of knights. He ordered the men of one group to dismount. Then he personally led them forward to help the first group of knights. He still felt the best way to fight the Swiss was on foot. He did not believe that peasants could defeat nobles in armor.

But as Leopold led the second group of knights forward, the Austrian square broke apart. The knights threw down their lances and turned to run away. But clad in heavy armor, they moved slowly and clumsily. The Swiss caught them from behind and cut them down by the hundreds!

Now Swiss axmen and swordsmen rushed toward Duke Leopold and the second group of Austrians. The proud

The flags of five of the Swiss cantons that fought against Austria to keep their freedom.

knights realized that they, too, would be slaughtered. Like the others, they dropped their lances and tried to run. Seeing that the battle was lost, the knights still on horseback turned and galloped away before the Swiss could attack them!

And so, the Swiss won again. The common farmers, shepherds, and workmen had defeated the proud and haughty nobles and kept their freedom.

The girl who saved France

Orléans, France, 1429

The attack had failed. Bloody, weary, and in low spirits, throngs of French soldiers plodded back into the city.

Suddenly, a horse came clattering up a narrow, cobblestone street toward them. It was a magnificent white horse, and upon its back sat a rider in gleaming silvery armor, holding a great white and gold banner that whipped and snapped in the breeze.

"Turn around!" shouted the rider. "Go boldly against the English! We shall win!"

The soldiers halted. At the sight of the rider, they seemed to lose their weariness and low spirits and to become fresh and confident. Shouting

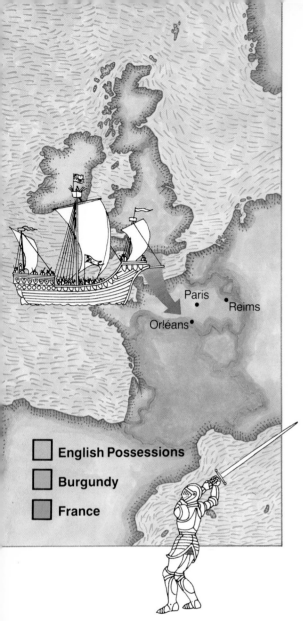

English Possessions

Burgundy

France

Paris

Reims

Orléans

eagerly, they turned around. With horse and rider moving with them, they rushed back out of the city toward the enemy!

It was the year 1429, and the rider on the white horse was the leader of the army of France—a seventeen-year-old girl, Jeanne d'Arc (zhahn dark), known in English as Joan of Arc!

At the beginning of the year 1429, the nation of France faced disaster. For nearly one hundred years, the French had fought invaders from England. But the English had won battle after battle and had conquered a large part of the country. Another part was under the rule of the Duke of Burgundy (BUR guhn dee), who had allied himself with the English. Only a small part of France was still in the hands of French nobles known as Armagnacs (ahr mah NYAHKS).

The English intended to conquer the lands held by the

Armagnac nobles. Then, most of France would belong to England, and the rest would be part of Burgundy. France would no longer be a free nation with its own king, as it had been for hundreds of years.

This portrait of Charles VII was made after he was crowned king of France.

Of course, the French were willing to fight for their freedom, but there was no one to lead them. The last king of France had died, and his son, Prince Charles, had not been crowned as the new king.

And it looked as if he would never become king. To be crowned, he would have to go to the city of Reims (reemz), where all kings of France were officially crowned. But an English army blocked the way to Reims. And Reims itself was in the hands of the soldiers of Burgundy. For Prince Charles to get to Reims, the French would have to defeat the English army. Then they would have to capture Reims from the Burgundians. This hardly seemed possible for the small French army that still existed.

Thus, France faced disaster. And the man who should have been France's leader was helpless. Then, suddenly, Joan of Arc appeared, and everything changed!

Joan was the daughter of a farmer who lived near the town of Domrémy. A sturdy, rather plain girl, she had black hair and dark eyes. Like most women of her time, she never went to school. She could neither read nor write. And until she was seventeen, she had never been away from the place where she was born. Yet, this plain, uneducated peasant girl became the leader of the French army and made it possible for Prince Charles to become king of France!

Joan of Arc's birthplace

The story of Joan of Arc seems like a fairy tale, yet it really happened. When she was a young girl, she began to hear voices that told her they were the voices of saints and angels. When she was seventeen, Joan claimed that Saint Catherine, Saint Margaret, and Saint Michael had appeared to her, telling her that she would help Charles be crowned king and would save France! They told her to go to the nobleman who was in charge of the district where she lived and he would send her to see the Prince.

When Joan first went to the nobleman with this strange story he simply laughed at her and sent her away. But she went back twice more. And the third time, the man gave her a horse and some soldiers to guard her, and sent her to Prince Charles. Some people think he only did this because he wanted to get rid of her. Others think he did it because he decided she might be useful to the prince in some way. And some say that Joan performed a miracle that convinced the man to do as she asked.

Joan had to ride a long way, through country that was full of English soldiers. To disguise herself, she cut her hair short and dressed like a boy.

Prince Charles lived in a castle, with a number of Armagnac noblemen and ladies. They had received a message about Joan's coming. The prince decided to test her, to find out if she was crazy or was indeed telling the truth. When Joan was brought in, the Prince, dressed like the other nobles, stood among them. One of the noblemen, pretending to

Joan said that Saint Michael appeared to her and told her that she would save France.

be the prince, sat on a fancy chair that looked like a throne. Everyone expected Joan to go to him, believing him to be Prince Charles. Then they would laughingly ask her why the saints hadn't told her the truth.

But when Joan came into the great hall of the castle, she gave the man in the chair only a passing glance. She began to move through the crowd, looking at men's faces. No one was quite sure whether someone had told her who was the prince or not, but when she caught sight of him, she walked straight to him and knelt down. "God give you long life, noble prince," she said in a soft, clear voice.

The prince tried to keep on with the test. "I am not the prince," he told her.

"Indeed you are, Sir, and no other," said Joan, her dark eyes shining up at him. "I have come with orders from God to help you and to help the kingdom. The King of Heaven orders that you shall be crowned at Reims!"

The prince and Joan moved away from the crowd and talked together for a time. No one knows what Joan told the prince, but it was said that as she talked a look of great joy came over his face. After that he put her in command of the French army, and acted as if he truly believed she could make him king and save his kingdom.

About two months after her meeting with the prince, Joan led a French force to the city of Orléans (awr lay AHN), which was surrounded by an English army. The English soldiers had built a ring of small forts around part of the city.

These blocked off most of the roads. However, there was a gap through which people could get in and out of the city. And the Loire (lwahr) River, which runs past Orléans, made it possible to get in and out of the city by boat.

Tales of Joan and her visions, and of strange and miraculous deeds she had done, had swept through France. It seemed to many French people as if God had taken their side. There was hardly a French soldier who didn't believe with all his heart that Joan was truly helped by Heaven.

The English soldiers and leaders had also heard of Joan. They, too, believed she had supernatural powers. But they didn't think those powers came from Heaven. The English believed Joan was a witch and got her power from the devil!

To the people of Orléans, Joan seemed like an angel who had come to their rescue. She wore a suit of silvery armor and carried a large flag. Thunderous cheers greeted her as she rode her big white warhorse through the city streets. People crowded about, just trying to touch her.

A few days after Joan's arrival, the
commander of the soldiers defending
Orléans launched an attack against one
of the English forts. Joan, who was
sleeping, suddenly sprang from her bed,
exclaiming that the voices of the saints
had awakened her. Quickly, she put on
her armor and mounted her horse.
Seizing her flag, she galloped through the
streets toward the sound of battle.

But the English had beaten off the
attack. The defeated French soldiers

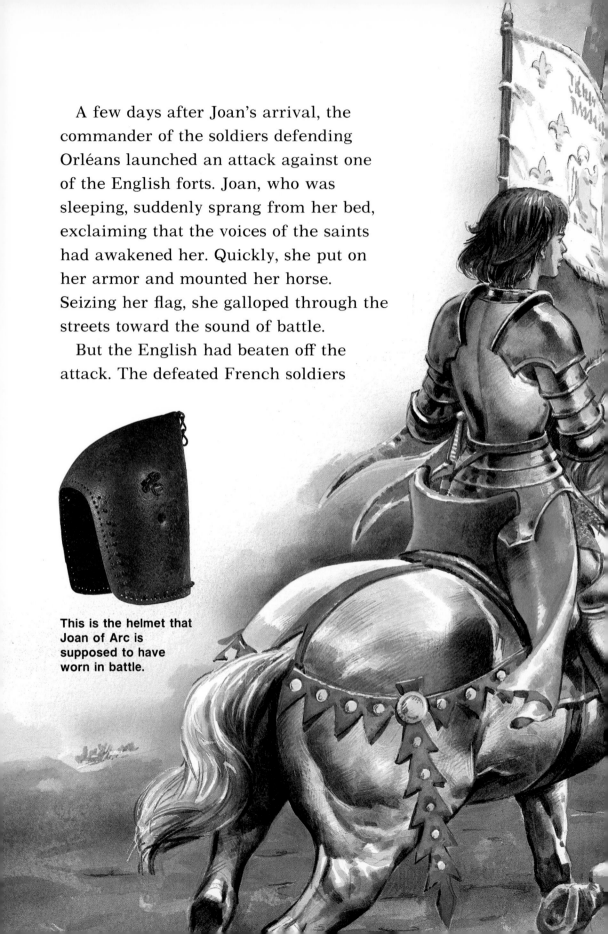

This is the helmet that
Joan of Arc is
supposed to have
worn in battle.

were trudging back into the city. Joan rode toward them, crying out that they should turn around and try again. She promised them they would win.

The spirits of the men were lifted as if by magic! They rushed back to the fort. This time the English could not hold them off. In a bloody battle, the French captured the fort. It was the first French victory in a long, long time.

Two days later, another attack was made on another fort. At first, things again went badly for the French. The

English came out of the fort, and in close fighting began to push the French back into the city.

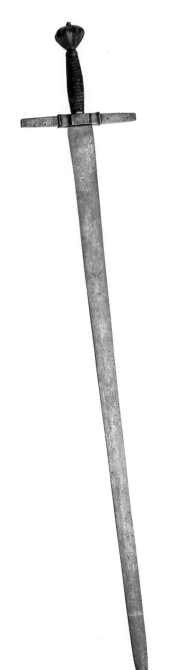

A sword of the kind used by both English and French soldiers.

The French and English soldiers were dressed and equipped almost exactly alike. They wore many different kinds of steel helmets, and some had short-sleeved jackets of chain mail. Most had leather jackets covered with little metal studs, or quilted jackets of canvas with a metal plate inside each quilted section. French soldiers often had white crosses sewn onto their jackets, and the English had red crosses.

Their weapons were swords, spears, long-handled axes, longbows, and crossbows. The string of a crossbow was pulled back with a crank and held in place with a hook. When a trigger was squeezed, the hook let go and the string snapped forward, shooting a small arrow. Some men had a hand-gun—a thick metal tube fastened on a long wooden stick. This weapon fired a heavy metal ball.

Joan saw that the French soldiers were being pushed back. Beside her was a sturdy French knight nicknamed "The

Angry One." Turning to him, Joan cried out, "In the Lord's name, let us charge these English!"

Together, man and girl galloped straight into the crowd of English soldiers. Scores of French soldiers rushed forward with them. The English retreated back into their fort, but the French broke in and captured the fort. Again, Joan had turned defeat into victory.

That night, the French made preparations to attack the strongest of the English forts the next day. It is said that Joan told the priest who was her chaplain that she would be wounded in the attack. "Blood will flow from my body above my chest," she said.

The attack began in the morning. French soldiers rushed forward, carrying ladders. These were placed against the fort's wall. While Frenchmen tried to scramble up the ladders, Englishmen at the top of the wall tried to push the

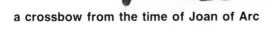

a crossbow from the time of Joan of Arc

ladders over. English crossbowmen and hand-gunners shot at the men on the ladders, and French bowmen and gunners shot at the English soldiers on the wall.

When Frenchmen managed to get to the top of the wall, they battled Englishmen with swords and axes. As Frenchmen fell off the wall, others sprang up and took their place. As ladders were pushed over, French soldiers rushed to put them up again. But the English fought like demons, and the French could not get into the fort. By afternoon the battle was still raging.

Joan was in the thick of it, urging men forward, helping with the ladders, calling encouragement. Suddenly she staggered back and fell to the ground. The men around her saw with horror that an arrow had gone through her neck!

A young French knight leaped from his horse and helped Joan into the saddle. A cheer went up from the English as they saw the horse, with Joan slumped over on its back, being led away.

Knights and soldiers took Joan to a quiet place, away from the battle. They placed her gently on the ground. The arrow had gone partway through the side of her neck, just above her shoulder. Joan's face was pale, and tears of pain ran down her cheeks, but she sat up and pulled the arrow out of her neck. Just as she had said, blood flowed out of her body, above her chest. The wound was treated with olive oil and beef fat, and the bleeding soon stopped.

One of the French leaders came to see how she was. "How does the battle go?" she asked.

He shook his head. "Not well, Joan. The men are tiring. We have been fighting for nearly thirteen hours now, and the cursed English seem as strong as ever." He hesitated a moment, then said, "I think we must give up."

"In God's name, do not!" she begged. "You will be in the fort soon, do not doubt it. I tell you that when you see my banner reach the wall again, the fort will be taken. For now, let the men rest awhile and eat."

After a moment, he agreed. Joan mounted her horse and rode a short distance up a hill. The French soldiers

Joan of Arc in full armor

moved back from the fort, out of range of English arrows and bullets. Sprawled on the grass, eating bread and cheese, they watched Joan. The red rays of the evening sun shone on her armor.

She rode back and dismounted. Because of her wound she now could not carry her banner. She gave it to a sturdy young soldier to carry, and started toward the fort. When the French soldiers saw the white banner moving forward a tremendous cheer went up. They arose, and like a vast wave went surging toward the fort.

This time, nothing could stop them. The English, who had thought Joan was

dead, seemed terrified. As she had said, when her banner reached the wall, the fort was doomed. French soldiers swarmed up the ladders by the hundreds, hurling themselves at the Englishmen defending the top of the wall, and poured into the fort.

The fort sat at the edge of the river, where there was a wooden bridge. French soldiers had guided a raft loaded with tar, barrels of olive oil, and greasy rags under the bridge and set it afire. As the bridge started to burn, the English, fearful of being trapped, began to flee across it. As the last of them were crossing, the bridge collapsed and scores of English soldiers were drowned.

And so, the strongest and most important of the English forts was now in French hands. Night had fallen, and in darkness Joan led the victorious French soldiers back into Orléans. News of their victory had reached the city, and it was ablaze with light and humming with noise. Huge crowds of cheering people carrying blazing torches greeted Joan and the soldiers. Throughout the city, church bells rang joyously.

The next day, the remaining English soldiers left their forts and marched away. Orléans had been saved, and every soldier and citizen knew it had been saved by Joan of Arc.

During the next four months, under Joan's leadership, the French army captured three cities and beat an English army in battle—the greatest French victory in ninety years. The way to Reims was opened, and Prince Charles was crowned king of France. The little farm girl, who had been laughed at for being foolish and crazy, had saved a city, beaten every English force she led her army against, and created a king!

But then, things seemed to go wrong for Joan. She failed to capture several cities she led her soldiers against. And in the attempt to take one of them, Joan was taken prisoner by Burgundian soldiers!

The Burgundians sent Joan to the commander of the English forces, the Duke of Bedford. He and other English leaders felt that if they proved Joan to be a witch, many French people would turn away from King Charles. They put her on trial for witchcraft. The trial was long and complicated, but it was all just a pretense—the English were determined that Joan should be found guilty, and so she was. On the morning of May 30, 1431, she was burned to death at the stake!

However, the plan of the English lords didn't work. Everyone knew the trial had been faked, and no one turned against King Charles. Instead, more and more people thought Joan was a heroine. In memory of her, the French people became united under their new king.

Charles made a treaty with the Burgundians, so his army was able to give full attention to the English

This drawing, done in the 1400's, shows an English soldier tying Joan of Arc to the stake.

This statue of Joan of Arc stands in Paris, the capital of France.

invaders. Slowly, the French began to push the English out of the places they had conquered. In a final battle in 1453, the French destroyed the last English army in France. After more than one hundred years, the last hope of the English to conquer France was gone. It was twenty-two years after Joan of Arc's death, but the French felt that it was because of what she had done that the invaders were finally driven out.

The defeat of the Armada

The English Channel
July 31-August 7, 1588

King Philip II of Spain was a dark-eyed man with a puffy lower lip and a small beard and mustache. He always dressed in black and almost never smiled. Everyone called him "Philip the Careful" because he never did anything without thinking about it for a long, long time. And in the early 1580's, Philip the Careful began to think about conquering the country of England.

Philip was quite sure that Spain could conquer England. Spain was the greatest power in the world. It ruled Portugal, much of Italy, and the Netherlands. It also owned vast, rich colonies in Central

a Spanish shipyard

and South America. These colonies supplied the gold, silver, and jewels that made Spain wealthy. The Spanish navy was large and powerful, and the Spanish army had won many victories. So, Spain did pretty much as it pleased.

England, however, was a tiny nation with no colonies and not much wealth. But it was the only nation of Europe willing to stand up to Spain. The English wanted some of the wealth Spain was taking from its American Colonies. The English and Spanish also had religious differences. Spain was a Roman Catholic country, and most of England was Protestant. So, for a long time, England and Spain had fought a kind of "cold war" against each other.

English ships sometimes attacked

Spanish treasure ships coming from the colonies. The English also raided towns in the colonies. English soldiers flocked to the Netherlands, to help Dutch Protestant rebels who were fighting to gain freedom from Spain. An English fleet had even raided a Spanish seaport and burned Spanish ships. In return, Spanish ships and soldiers kept English ships from carrying wool to Europe to sell. This made England desperately poor, because it depended upon its wool for most of its money.

But now, King Philip decided the time had come to settle things with England once and for all. He worked out a plan to

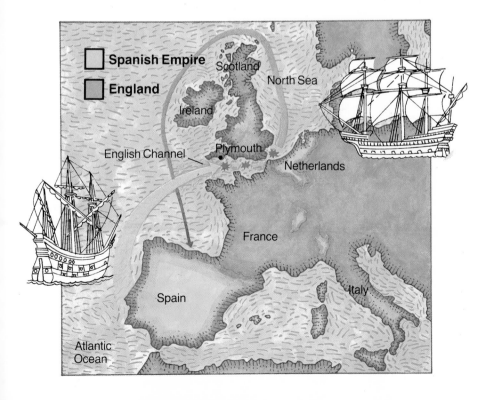

King Philip II of Spain planning the invasion of England.

launch a gigantic invasion of England by a great armada (ahr MAH duh), or large fleet of warships. Transport ships carrying thousands of soldiers would sail across the English Channel, protected by dozens of warships. The warships would destroy any English ships that might try to fight them. Then the army would land in England and conquer it. Philip would become its king and rule it with an iron hand. And one of the first things he intended to do was make the English change their religion!

Queen Elizabeth I of England as she appeared at the time of the Armada.

Throughout Spain, workers began to make the Armada ready for the invasion. Old ships were cleaned and repaired. New ships were built. Many cannons were made and huge quantities of gunpowder were mixed. Enormous numbers of weapons were manufactured.

Of course, the English soon learned what was planned. The English ruler was a red-haired, hot-tempered queen named Elizabeth. She and the English leaders began to make plans to fight off the Spanish invasion.

Elizabeth and her leaders knew that if the powerful Spanish army landed in England, an English army probably wouldn't be able to defeat it. But if enough Spanish ships could be destroyed at sea, the Spanish army would never get to England. So the English determined that their battle for freedom would have to be fought on the water—a sea battle.

A Spanish warship (above) of the kind that sailed in the Armada and (left) a Spanish soldier.

Sea battles at this time were fought by wooden sailing ships with two or three masts that held several big cloth sails. The ships had rows of cannons on each side. These cannons fired heavy iron balls weighing as much as fifty pounds (22.5 kilograms) as far as several thousand yards (meters). However, the English and Spanish sailors had different ideas about how a sea battle should be fought. And they disagreed about what kind of ship was the best warship.

An English warship of the kind that defeated the Spanish Armada.

The Spanish ships, called galleons, were big and bulky, with high sides. Their guns were set up high so they could fire onto the deck of an enemy ship and wipe out much of its crew. The Spanish idea was to move in close, firing at the enemy ship's deck, until the two ships actually touched. Then, Spanish soldiers would swarm onto the enemy ship, battling with swords and long-handled axes to capture it.

The English idea was completely different. Their galleons were slimmer, lower, and lighter. And their guns shot a lighter ball for a longer distance. They were faster than the Spanish ships.

Instead of getting close, English seamen believed in staying a long distance away from an enemy ship and smashing it up with cannonballs. With their quickness, English ships could dodge and turn to keep an enemy ship from getting an accurate shot.

Just as the Spanish were doing, the English began cleaning and repairing their warships for the great sea battle that would come. They worked day and night, working by the light of torches in the darkness. They had no idea when the Armada would come, but they had to be ready for it. By the spring of 1588, the English fleet of fifty-four ships was in perfect shape.

This was none too soon, for on May 28 the Spanish Armada set sail. It was the biggest war fleet ever put together in Europe up to that time. There were 20 big galleons, 40 big merchant ships that had been equipped with cannons, 34 light, fast, scout ships, and many others—130 ships in all. With flags snapping from the tops of the masts, the ships of the Armada sailed from Lisbon and began to move slowly north along the coast of Spain.

But this was not the entire invasion force. The Spanish army that was to conquer England, and the ships that were to carry it, waited on the coast of the Netherlands. King Philip had ordered the Armada to join the army ships. Then the entire force would sail across the English Channel against England.

But things were not going to work out quite as King Philip had planned. The English had a number of fast ships out watching for the approach of the Armada. Long before the Armada reached the Netherlands, one of these ships spotted it. Immediately, the ship turned and raced back to England with the news.

The English fleet was anchored off the seaport of Plymouth. On the day the scout ship returned, most of the ship captains were playing the game of lawn bowling in a park. They laughed and chatted, enjoying themselves as they took turns rolling a large, dark wooden ball at a small white one.

There was a sudden clatter as a horseman galloped up the cobblestone street that ran past the bowling green. He reined his horse to a stop, jumped from its back, and hurried toward the bowlers. "My Lord Admiral," he called. "My Lord Admiral."

Lord Charles Howard, who had been appointed admiral of the English fleet by Queen Elizabeth, went to meet the man. They spoke for a time. Then, Admiral Howard turned back to the bowlers and announced that the Spanish

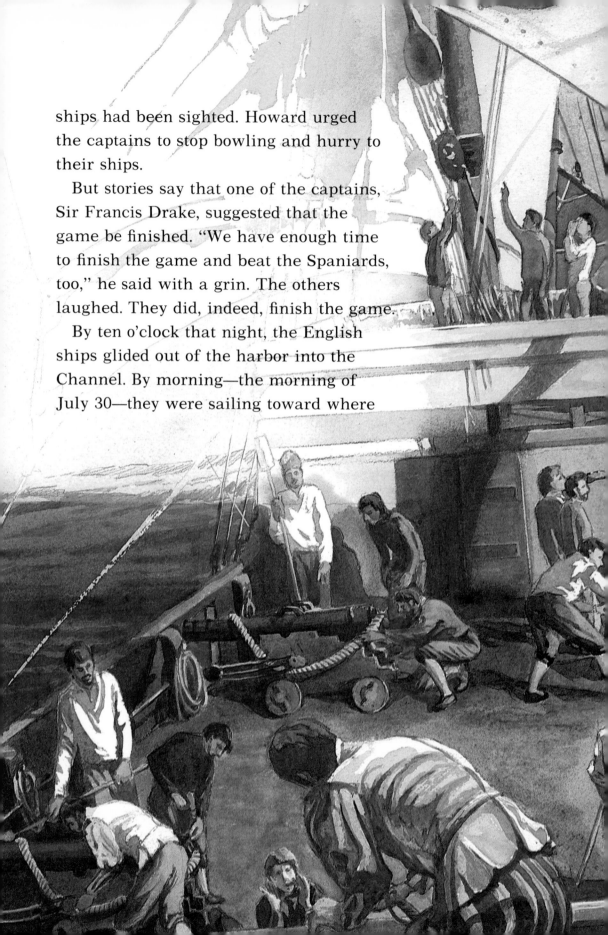

ships had been sighted. Howard urged
the captains to stop bowling and hurry to
their ships.

But stories say that one of the captains,
Sir Francis Drake, suggested that the
game be finished. "We have enough time
to finish the game and beat the Spaniards,
too," he said with a grin. The others
laughed. They did, indeed, finish the game.

By ten o'clock that night, the English
ships glided out of the harbor into the
Channel. By morning—the morning of
July 30—they were sailing toward where

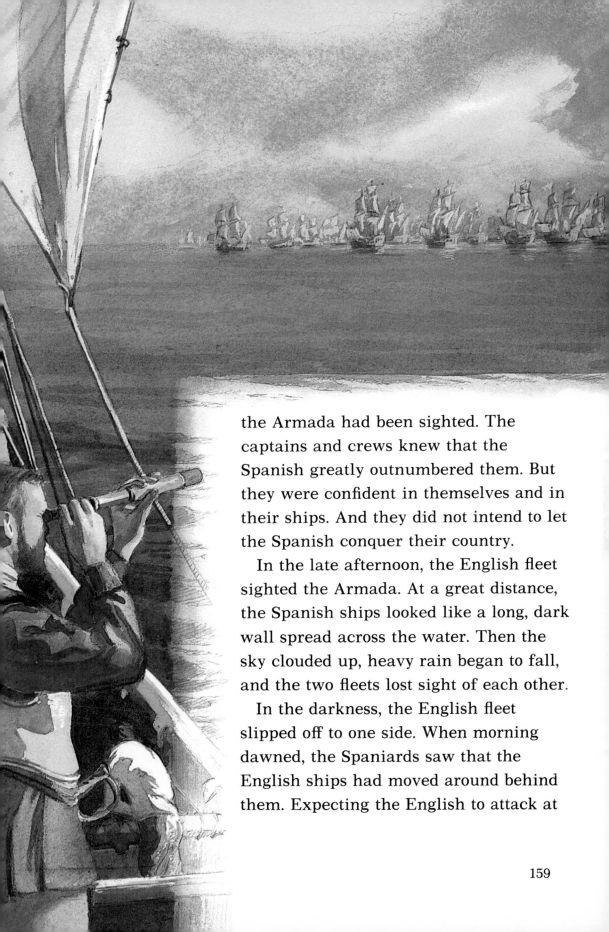

the Armada had been sighted. The captains and crews knew that the Spanish greatly outnumbered them. But they were confident in themselves and in their ships. And they did not intend to let the Spanish conquer their country.

In the late afternoon, the English fleet sighted the Armada. At a great distance, the Spanish ships looked like a long, dark wall spread across the water. Then the sky clouded up, heavy rain began to fall, and the two fleets lost sight of each other.

In the darkness, the English fleet slipped off to one side. When morning dawned, the Spaniards saw that the English ships had moved around behind them. Expecting the English to attack at

This old map shows the Spanish Armada in a crescent formation, with the English fleet in hot pursuit.

The Duke of Medina Sidonia was the commander of the Spanish Armada.

once, the Spanish admiral had a cannon fire a signal shot. The Spanish ships arranged themselves in a crescent formation, like the shape of a quarter moon, and continued sailing into the Channel.

With that, a moving battle began that continued for the next six days. The Armada kept sailing for the Netherlands, to join the waiting Spanish army. And all the time groups of English ships attacked different parts of the crescent formation. As cannons thundered, two badly damaged Spanish ships did surrender, but not much else happened. It was clear that the English ships were faster and could shoot farther. But the Spanish formation seemed impossible to break.

Admiral Howard grew worried. His ships had used up a lot of gunpowder and cannonballs but hadn't really accomplished anything. The Armada still headed steadily toward its goal.

The Spanish admiral, the Duke of Medina Sidonia (mah DEE nah see DOHN yah), was also worried. His ships, too, had used up a lot of ammunition. They had hardly enough left to fight a major battle if the English should attack. So, when the Armada came to a sheltered spot off the coast of France, the admiral ordered all the ships to drop anchor. He intended to buy more ammunition from the French. He also wanted to send a message to the commander of the Spanish army.

Seeing what the Spanish did, Admiral Howard ordered his ships to drop anchor, too. The two fleets lay unmoving, not much more than a mile (1.6 kilometers) apart. Admiral Howard called a meeting of all his captains to decide what they should do. They came up with a daring plan.

Around midnight, two days later, lookouts on the Spanish ships saw a row of lights suddenly appear where the English fleet was anchored. As the lights grew in size, the Spaniards realized that a number of blazing ships, close together,

Lord Charles Howard commanded the English fleet that defeated the Armada.

were headed straight for the Spanish fleet! The English had sacrificed eight of their vessels to make fireships. They had stuffed the ships with anything that would burn, steered them toward the Armada, and then set them on fire.

Some of the smaller, faster Spanish ships, placed around the Armada as guards, tried to head off the fireships. They did manage to push two toward shore, where they burned harmlessly in shallow water. But the remaining six, now masses of flame, floated in among the anchored ships of the Armada.

The Spanish ships were close together. A single fire ship drifting among them could set dozens afire. Panic overwhelmed the Spanish captains. Fearing even to take the time to raise their anchors, many simply had the anchor ropes cut so their ships could quickly move out of danger. The Armada began to break up into clusters of ships heading in all directions.

In the darkness, the English captains could not see what was happening. But it did not look to them as if their fire ships were doing much damage. They couldn't

see any fires breaking out among the
Spanish ships. They feared that when
morning came they would have to sail in
close and attack the Armada. Badly
outnumbered, they would be at a
disadvantage.

But when the sky finally grew light
enough, the English were overjoyed to see
that the Armada had scattered over miles
of water. It did not look as if the
Spaniards could ever get back into their
close, crescent formation. Now they
would be at the mercy of the faster
English vessels with their long-range
guns!

Quickly, the English ships hauled up
their anchors. Sails spread to catch the
wind, they sped forward to attack the
enemy. From sunrise until four o'clock in
the afternoon, the English Channel

resounded with the steady thunder of
cannon fire as English ships moved in
and out among the Spaniards, pounding
them with cannonballs.

An English ship would sail toward a
Spanish ship until it was almost within
range of the Spanish guns. Then the
English ship would turn so that one side
faced the Spaniard. On command, all the
guns on that side would fire. Such a
broadside sent dozens of cannonballs
screaming through the air to smash into
the Spanish ship's wooden sides, rip up
its deck, break its masts, tear holes in its
sails, and kill or wound its crew.

The Spanish guns couldn't shoot as far as the English ones, and the Spanish were nearly out of cannonballs. So, the Spanish ships tried desperately to get close enough to the English ships so that soldiers could board them. But the quick-moving English ships always managed to keep their distance.

By late afternoon, the English ships had used up most of their ammunition. As they began to move away from the Spanish ships, the battle slowly came to an end. A few English ships were slightly damaged, but the Armada was in dreadful shape.

The English had forced one of the biggest and finest of the Spanish ships onto rocks near the shore and captured it. Two other ships were so badly damaged they had drifted helplessly into shallow water and become stuck in sand. Still another was leaking so badly that it slowly sank. And almost all the others were terribly battered and leaking, with many of their crewmen dead or injured.

The Spanish admiral and all the captains knew that the Armada could not fight another battle. It would never be able to fight its way past the English fleet, to get to where the Spanish army was waiting. The chance to invade England was gone. The Armada had failed.

The Spaniards' only thought now was to try to get home. But they couldn't go back the way they had come, for the English fleet blocked the way. They had to sail northward, then turn and sail all the way around Scotland and Ireland. It was a long, terrible voyage! The ships ran out of food and water long before they reached Spain, and hundreds of sick and injured sailors died. Many of the battered,

leaking ships sank on the way. Of the 130 ships that had left Spain, only 67 got back.

The danger to England was over. After the loss of so many ships, Spain did not have the strength to invade England. But the danger had been great. Had the Spanish army reached England, it probably would have conquered the country. King Philip would have ruled England harshly and forced the English people to give up their chosen religion.

By keeping the Armada from joining with the Spanish army, the English fleet saved its country. England had depended upon the speed and weapons of its ships, and the courage and skill of their captains and crews. All these things had kept England free.

The frightened city

The siege of Vienna, Austria
July 14-September 12, 1683

Fear filled the people in the city of Vienna (vee EHN uh). They went about their daily business with grim, worried faces. There were no jokes and little if any laughter. Everyone knew that a vast army was moving toward Vienna—and that army could bring death or slavery to every person in the city!

Vienna was the capital of a group of central European countries that formed what is known as the Holy Roman Empire. The empire consisted of what are now Austria, Czechoslovakia, parts of Germany and Italy, and the Netherlands. Vienna stood like a gateway at the southernmost

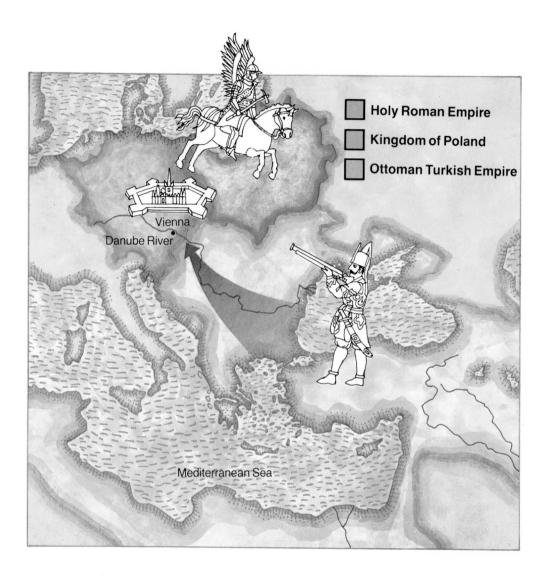

Holy Roman Empire

Kingdom of Poland

Ottoman Turkish Empire

Vienna

Danube River

Mediterranean Sea

edge of the Holy Roman Empire. Nearby, was the northernmost tip of a much larger empire, the Turkish Empire.

For hundreds of years the Turkish Empire had spread throughout the Near East and into southeastern Europe. It had conquered Greece and much of the lands that are now Bulgaria, Albania, Romania,

Yugoslavia, and Hungary. It had finally come to a stop at the border of Austria.

Turkish emperors had long dreamed of sending their armies into Austria and central Europe. They dearly wanted to make those lands part of their empire. However, to do that, the Turks had to capture Vienna first. This great city stood in the middle of a broad valley surrounded by mountains, with the Danube River flowing past it. The Turks could not just go around it. They would have to take control of it and use it as a base for their invasion.

They had tried to capture Vienna in 1529, but had failed. Now, in the year 1683, they were going to try again. A huge army of about 150,000 Turkish soldiers was marching up the Danube toward the city.

And well might this army strike fear into the people of Vienna! It included thousands of Tartars (TAHR tuhrz)—wild, savage horsemen known for their cruelty and delight in destruction. There were also horsemen known as "crazy heads," who would take any risk and brave any danger in order to defeat their enemies.

And there were the terrifying foot soldiers known as Janissaries (JAN uh sehr eez). They were sworn to wipe out all Christians. Like most of the men of the Turkish army, they were Muslims (MUZ luhmz) and followed the religion of Islam (IHS luhm). They hated all Christians.

News of the Turkish attack caught the emperor and the leaders of the Holy Roman Empire by surprise. Their soldiers were scattered throughout the empire. They could quickly scrape together only a small number of fighting men—twenty-eight thousand foot soldiers and fourteen thousand horsemen. The Turks outnumbered this little army nearly four to one. The army's commander, the Duke of Lorraine (luh RAYN), did not dare try to stop the Turkish advance. He took the army into the hills beyond Vienna and waited for help to come.

More help had been promised. The kingdom of Poland lay next to Austria. If the Turks conquered Austria, they were sure to attack Poland next. The Holy Roman Emperor, Leopold I, sent a

a Turkish "crazy head"

a Turkish soldier

a Turkish Janissary

an Austrian cavalryman

173

message to the Polish king, John Sobieski (saw BYEHS kee), urging that they join forces against the Turks. Sobieski agreed to send an army of forty thousand men to help save Vienna.

Meanwhile, Vienna made ready for attack. Count Starhemberg (SHTAH rehm behrk), commander of the eleven thousand soldiers who would defend the city, did what was necessary, no matter what the cost. The high, thick wall around the city needed repairing in places. Whole streets were torn up to provide stones for the wall. To protect against fire, Starhemberg had the wooden

roofs taken off all the houses near the wall. And he had most of the houses and buildings outside the wall burned to the ground so that the Turks would have no place to take cover when they attacked.

Scores of cannons were brought into the city. Cranes lifted them onto rooftops, where they could fire over the city wall. Tons and tons of gunpowder were brought in and stored in cellars throughout the city.

Day and night, a steady parade of horse-drawn carts and wagons rumbled through the city gates. They were filled with bags of grain, casks of beer and wine, barrels of dried and pickled meats and fish, cheeses, and other food. Starhemberg wanted to store up enough food to keep the people of the city fed for as long as possible. Once the Turks arrived and surrounded the city, there would be no way of getting more food.

Day and night, soldiers stood watch on the city walls, gazing south for signs of the Turks. On July 12, 1683, the guards saw distant clouds of smoke rising into the sky. The Turks were coming, and burning villages as they came! Quickly, the city gates were closed, barred, and walled up with stones.

When the sun rose the next day, a forest of tents surrounded the city. The Turks had arrived and made camp. The attack on Vienna was about to begin.

On July 14, the commander of the Turkish army, Kara Mustafa (MOOS tah fah), sent a message to Count Starhemberg. If the people of Vienna would agree to give up Christianity and become Muslims, or if they agreed to surrender the city and become part of the Turkish Empire, they would be spared. Otherwise—death or slavery for everyone!

In the name of the people of Vienna, Count Starhemberg refused. And so, Vienna found itself under siege (seej)—surrounded by an army determined to break through its walls and capture it.

Kara Mustafa had decided to try to blow up a section of the city wall, making an opening for his soldiers to swarm through. His plan was to have men dig a hole under a wall and fill it with a huge amount of gunpowder that would be set off with a fuse. But to do their digging,

a painting showing the siege of Vienna

the men had to get to the wall without being wiped out by gunfire and cannonfire. So Mustafa ordered trenches to be dug to the walls, to give the men protection.

Slowly, the trenches crept toward the walls. The Turks fired into the city with the 250 cannons they had brought. The Austrians fired back with the cannons mounted on rooftops throughout the city. Sometimes these cannons fired heavy, solid balls of metal that could smash a person's body. Other times, they shot hollow balls filled with powder, which exploded and sent scores of sharp metal fragments whizzing through the air.

For weeks the Turks worked at digging trenches to the walls. As the days passed, life became harder and harder for the people of Vienna. The stores of food began to run out, both for people and for the thousands of horses in the city. Many people and horses were killed every day by cannonfire, and there was soon no place to bury them. The streets became filled with garbage that could not be taken out of the city. Disease began to break out.

And, of course, there was still the constant fear that the Turks would finally

capture the city and slaughter everyone
in it. Was help really coming, people
wondered. Would Sobieski keep his
promise to bring an army to Vienna's
aid? Even if he did—would he and the
Duke of Lorraine arrive in time to save
the city?

At last, the Turkish trenches reached
the walls. Now began the work of digging
beneath the walls. On August 3, the
Turks blew up a small section of wall
and tried to storm their way in. A hail of
musket balls from the guns of the
Austrian soldiers drove them back. Both

an Austrian musket

the Turks and Austrians had muskets—guns that fired a single lead ball at a time and took a long time to load.

More weeks went by, during which the Turks managed to push through several parts of the wall. But the Austrians put up barricades—new sections of wall made of paving stones—that kept the Turks out of the city. There were small battles each day, as the Turks tried to get through these barricades and the Austrians fought to keep them out.

Within the city, things got worse and worse. Food was so scarce that people ate dogs and cats—when they could get them. The water became polluted, and many people died from the terrible disease called dysentery. When would help come, everyone wondered.

On September 4, the thundering roar of a huge explosion startled the people of Vienna. Everyone rushed into the streets, staring anxiously in the direction of the wall.

"What is it?" shrieked a woman. "What has happened?"

"Look there!" shouted a man. He pointed at a giant, swirling cloud of smoke that was rising over the housetops.

The Turks had blown a gigantic hole in the wall. By the hundreds, the Turks rushed toward it with shouts of "Allah! Allah!" (the Muslim name for God). Austrian soldiers sped toward the opening and poured a deadly hail of musket fire into the charging enemy.

Turks went down by the scores, but more kept coming, and many managed to reach the Austrians. They hacked and chopped at them with swords and axes. The Austrians fought back, using their muskets as clubs. Or they stabbed at their enemies with pikes—long, sharp spears. The battle raged at the opening in the wall for two hours. Finally, unable to break through, the

a Turkish sword

Turks pulled back and retreated into their trenches.

Vienna was still free—but for how long? There were only four thousand soldiers left to defend the city, and they were worn out from fighting every day. Several thousand citizens also fought to defend their city, but they could not fight as well as the soldiers. Everyone knew that the Turks would soon break into the city. Unless help came very soon, Vienna was doomed!

All through July, the Polish king, John Sobieski, had been gathering his army. By the beginning of August he had fourteen thousand horsemen and thirteen thousand foot soldiers. He led his army toward Vienna.

The Polish foot soldiers were armed with muskets and huge axes. The horsemen wore helmets and had armor on the upper part of their body. They carried long lances and curved swords. Some of these horsemen were known as "winged hussars" (hu ZAHRZ) because they wore tall wings made of wood and feathers strapped to their backs. When these men galloped toward an enemy, their wings made a whirring sound that generally frightened enemy horses and made them hard to control. The wings also helped protect the men's backs from sword slashes.

By the end of August, Sobieski had joined the Duke of Lorraine in the hills west of Vienna. Shortly, two small armies from the German countries of Bavaria and Saxony, which were part of the Holy Roman Empire, joined them. Like most Austrians, most of these men were Christians. They knew that if they could not stop the Turks at Vienna, their homelands would soon be invaded. Then their people would lose not only their freedom but probably would be forced to change their religion.

The Duke of Lorraine and the Bavarian and Saxon commanders urged Sobieski to take command of the united army. He agreed. "We will attack the Turks at once," he told the others.

Led by Sobieski, the Christian army, which now numbered about sixty thousand men, moved down out of the hills, toward Vienna.

Kara Mustafa knew of this, for he had

a Polish foot soldier

a Polish cavalryman

scouts out watching for any sign of the Christian army. But instead of making his whole army ready to fight off the attack, he sent only his cavalry to fight Sobieski's army. Mustafa wanted to keep the main part of his army ready for an attack on Vienna. He felt sure the city was now too weak to keep the Turks out. He thought his cavalry alone could defeat the Christian army coming to save the city.

The Tartars, "crazy heads," and other Turkish horsemen also felt confident as they rode toward the oncoming Christians. Out in front of the Christian army was a force of thousands of German and Austrian horsemen. Early on the morning of September 12, the two cavalry forces sighted one another. Instantly, Muslims and Christians galloped at each other with slashing swords and thrusting lances. The battle was on!

The Turks soon began to get the worst of it. Grimly determined to drive these invaders out of their lands, the Austrians and Germans began to push the Turks back toward Vienna. This enabled

This painting, done about one hundred years after the siege, shows John Sobieski entering Vienna in triumph.

Sobieski to move dozens of cannons into place to begin firing into the Turkish camp.

Kara Mustafa suddenly realized that his whole army was in danger. He could see the Austrian, German, and Polish soldiers pouring down out of the wooded hills like a flood! Quickly, he gave orders. Drums began to thump and horns to shriek, calling the Turkish army together. Mustafa formed his men into a huge, thick mass.

For hours, cannons on both sides thundered and the steady banging of muskets filled the air. Several times, the Polish and Holy Roman Empire foot soldiers pushed all the way up to the Turkish front line, firing as they came. But each time they had to retreat, unable to break into the thick Turkish formation. However, the Turks lost many men, and their formation grew weaker.

At five o'clock in the afternoon, Sobieski decided the Turks had been weakened enough for a gigantic cavalry attack. He formed the Polish, German, and Austrian horsemen into many lines, with the Polish winged hussars in the

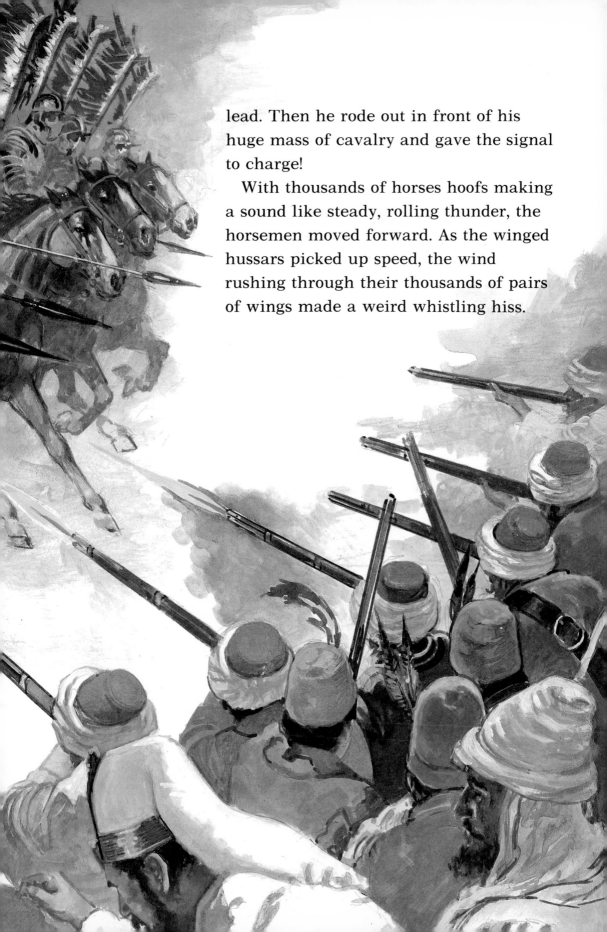

lead. Then he rode out in front of his
huge mass of cavalry and gave the signal
to charge!

With thousands of horses hoofs making
a sound like steady, rolling thunder, the
horsemen moved forward. As the winged
hussars picked up speed, the wind
rushing through their thousands of pairs
of wings made a weird whistling hiss.

The winged hussars lowered their lances as they crashed into the front line of Turks. Many hussars and horses were shot, but many hundreds of Turkish soldiers went down beneath the lances of the hussars. The whole mass of Turkish soldiers staggered and swayed from the shock of thousands of horses crashing into its front.

Many of the Polish hussars had broken or dropped their lances. Now they drew their curved swords and began to hack and slash at their enemies. The Austrian and German horsemen also forced their horses in among the Turkish foot soldiers, their swords rising and falling.

With Christian cavalrymen slashing at them, the Turkish soldiers had neither the time nor the room to load their muskets. Many of them simply used their guns as clubs. Others threw away their muskets and drew their swords. But the Turkish foot soldiers were no match for armored men on horses pushing in among them with slashing swords. As the Turks realized this, many of them grew afraid.

At the rear of the Turkish formation, men began to turn and run—by the dozens, then by the hundreds, then by the thousands. The Turkish army broke apart. In moments, every Turkish soldier was running for his life!

The battle was over and Vienna was safe. The Turkish army lost more than ten thousand men, while the Poles, Austrians, and Germans lost two thousand. They had kept central Europe and the Holy Roman Empire free. Never again would a Turkish emperor dare try to capture Vienna and conquer Europe.

The woman who fought for

The Battle of Monmouth
New Jersey, June 28, 1778

BLAM!

The big cannon thundered, spitting out a burst of fire and a cloud of thick, white smoke. A heavy iron cannonball sliced through the air toward the red-coated soldiers in the distance. Seconds later, the seven men of the gun crew were at work making the cannon ready to fire again.

"Sponge piece!" ordered Corporal Pell, who commanded the crew.

John Hays dipped his rammer, a pole with a stiff brush at one end, into a bucket of water. Then he shoved the dripping brush into the cannon barrel, swabbing it out. This would put out any sparks

liberty

or bits of glowing gunpowder that might still be burning inside.

"Handle cartridge!" commanded the corporal.

George McCauley hurried forward with a bag of gunpowder, while Jabez Peavy brought another iron cannonball. McCauley pushed the powder bag into the barrel and Jabez shoved the ball in after it.

"Charge piece!" said the corporal.

With the rammer, John Hays pushed the ball and bag all the way down the tube.

"Prime!" commanded the corporal. The gunner pushed a long, thick needle into the hole on the upper part of the gun barrel. This poked a hole in the powder bag inside. The gunner then shoved a long piece of hollow quill, from a bird feather, into the hole and down into the powder bag. Quickly, he filled the quill with powder from a box hanging at his waist.

"Fire!"

A burning rope, wrapped around a thin rod, was touched to the powder-filled quill. The powder in the quill caught fire and the fire raced down into the powder in the bag.

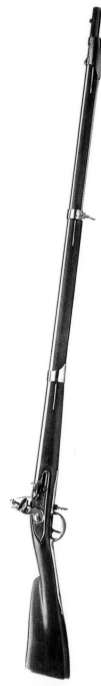

a Revolutionary War flintlock musket

This Revolutionary War cannon overlooks Valley Forge, where the American Army spent the winter of 1777–1778.

BLAM!

Again the cannon roared and jumped as the powder in the bag exploded. The explosion sent the ball hurtling out of the cannon so fast it couldn't be seen.

For hours, the men of the gun crew had fired their cannon over and over again, as fast as they could. The American Army was in a desperate battle and badly needed all their efforts.

It was the year 1778, and the American War for Independence was starting its fourth year. During the last three years, the American army commanded by George Washington had been badly defeated in several battles. It had just spent a terrible winter encamped at Valley Forge, where thousands of men died of cold, hunger, and disease.

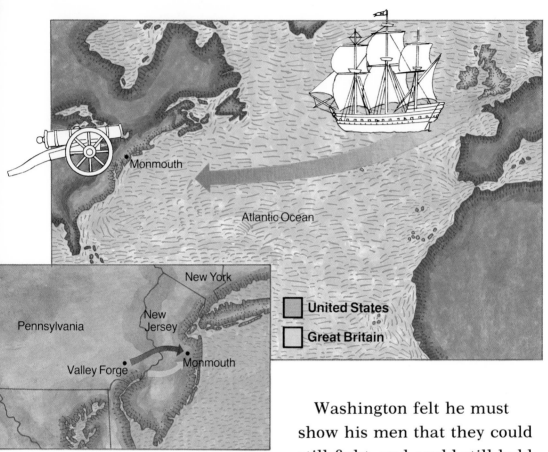

Monmouth

Atlantic Ocean

☐ **United States**
☐ **Great Britain**

New York

New Jersey

Pennsylvania

Valley Forge

Monmouth

Washington felt he must show his men that they could still fight, and could still hold their own against the enemy. So, he had deliberately attacked the British army of General Sir Henry Clinton as it marched toward New York. Washington was well aware of the risk. He knew that defeat could mean the end of the Americans' dream of freedom for their land.

But the British fought back

hard. They now hurled attack after attack against the Americans, determined to force them to retreat. If they could defeat the American army again, and it did have to retreat, the Americans would surely lose heart and their whole army might come apart.

It was a fiercely hot June day, with a temperature of 96° Fahrenheit (35.6° Celsius). The gunners, working hard in the heat, sweated heavily, and this made them very thirsty.

"Land o' Goshen, it's hot," gasped Jabez Peavy as he lifted another cannonball. "Molly," he called, "kin I have a drink?"

A young woman crouched some distance from the cannon rose to her feet and hurried toward him. She carried a large pitcher and a tin cup. Pouring water from the pitcher into the cup, she handed the cup to Jabez.

The young woman's name was Mary Hays. She was the wife of John Hays, the man who swabbed out the cannon and pushed powder and ball into it with the rammer. When the American Colonies had gone to war to gain their freedom and independence from Great Britain,

John had joined the American Army
and Mary had gone with him. Many
American wives had accompanied their
husbands when they went to fight for
independence.

Mary would truly have liked to be a
soldier as John was. She was willing to
fight for liberty for the colonies. But
women were not allowed to be soldiers,
so Mary helped out by cooking, sewing,
and cleaning for John and the other men
of the gun crew. And today she helped by
making trips to a nearby spring to keep
the thirsty men supplied with water.

Jabez drained the cup to the last drop. "Ah, that's good!" he exclaimed. "Thank heaven for Molly Pitcher!"

Mary smiled. Women named Mary were often called Molly, as a nickname. But because Mary was bringing them water in her pitcher, the men of the gun crew had given her the special nickname of Molly Pitcher.

She shook the pitcher. "It's nearly empty," she murmured. "I'd better go fill it again."

She set out at a trot for the spring. Around her, the noisy sounds of battle filled the air. There was a steady clamor of thousands of men talking and yelling, and a constant loud popping of muskets being fired. Somewhere, drums thudded out a steady *rat-a-tat-a-tat-a,* and there was a frequent crash of cannons. The air was thick with smoke, which added to the heat and discomfort.

George Washington
urges on his troops
at the Battle of
Monmouth.

Mary knew she was in danger. All
around her, musket balls ripped through
the air. At any moment she might be hit
by one. Or, a big, heavy cannonball could
come rushing through the air and smash
her body to pulp! But she wasn't
frightened. She simply did what she had
to do, and took her chances. She was not
the sort of person to hide from danger.

At the spring she paused for a moment
to bathe her face with cool water. Then
she filled her pitcher and hurried back to
the cannon. But as she neared it, she saw

that something was wrong. Samuel Hotten, the man who fired the cannon, was down on the ground. He was not moving and he was covered with blood. The other men were bent over him.

"He's hurt bad," Mary heard Corporal Pell say. "We've got to get him to the doctors. Yancey, can ye carry him?"

Mary went to her husband. "What happened, John?"

"He was hit by a musket ball," John told her. "I fear he'll not live." Mary watched, sadly, as the wounded man was carried off.

"Come on boys, let's get back to work," urged the corporal. "There are only five of us to man the gun now, so we've got to work harder."

Mary crouched down nearby as they went back to the steady task of firing the gun. The sound of hoofs made her look up. An officer on a sweating horse came galloping toward the cannon.

"The redcoats are attacking General Wayne's brigade," he yelled to Corporal Pell. "Direct your fire over the heads of Wayne's men to help break up the attack." As the horse galloped off again,

the sweating men swung the cannon around to point in the direction the officer had indicated. Mary stood up. Yes, she could see the long lines of red-coated British soldiers moving toward the lines of American soldiers of General Wayne's brigade.

This was how battles were fought in 1778. Many groups of five hundred or six hundred men formed into long lines, three rows deep. With beating drums to keep them in step, and carefully keeping their lines straight, the men making an attack would march steadily toward the enemy. The men being attacked stood in their lines, firing musket volleys—every man firing at the same time, so that hundreds of musket balls whistled toward the attackers.

Scores of the attackers might be hit by musket balls, and dozens might be smashed by cannonballs that came hurtling among them. If the attackers lost too many men, they might turn and retreat. But Mary could see that many groups, or regiments, of British soldiers were being sent against Wayne's brigade. Even if some were driven off, the others

might reach the American lines—and
then it might be the Americans who
would have to retreat!

Something came whooshing through
the air and smacked into the ground off
to one side. It was a cannonball. Mary
watched it bounce along for a way. The
British cannons were also firing over the
heads of their advancing regiments. That
meant more cannonballs would be
coming toward Corporal Pell and his gun
crew. We'll be in a lot more danger here
now, thought Mary.

An instant later there was a splintering
crack as a cannonball smashed into a

nearby tree. The ball tore loose a heavy branch and sent it hurtling through the air like a spear. Just missing Mary, the branch struck cannoneer Mapes with a thud. He was knocked to the ground, screaming with pain.

Mary ran to him. "My leg's broken," he said through gritted teeth. Mary helped George McCauley drag him out of the way. She sat beside him while the others kept firing the gun.

They were working as fast as they could, but there were only four of them now. It took longer to make each shot. Sweat poured off their bodies and they panted with their efforts.

Suddenly, to her horror, Mary saw her husband stagger back and fall to the ground!

"John!" she shrieked. "Are ye wounded?"

She rushed to his side and dropped to her knees beside him. She was relieved to see that he was breathing, but his eyes were closed and he was deathly pale. When she touched his cheek, his skin felt cold and clammy.

"Oh, Johnny, don't die," she wept.

Actually, John Hays hadn't been wounded. The hard work in the terrible heat had been too much. He was suffering from what doctors call heat exhaustion. He had only fainted, but Mary feared he was dying.

The gunners were shouting to one another over the noise of the battle. "We can't keep the gun going," yelled Jabez Peavy. "There aren't enough of us."

"We must do our best," said Corporal Pell. "They need us!"

Mary realized that with John gone, there weren't enough men to fire the gun at a good, steady rate. She scrambled to her feet.

"I can help," she yelled. "I know what to do!" She picked up her husband's rammer.

Corporal Pell stared at her. "But—but you're a gal!" he exclaimed. The idea of a woman fighting in a battle seemed to shock him.

This painting shows Molly Pitcher in action at the Battle of Monmouth. In the background, George Washington can be seen on horseback.

"That doesn't matter," she told him angrily.

"Let her do it, corporal," urged George McCauley. "A woman ought to be able to fight for liberty too, if she wants!"

"By thunder, I reckon you're right," decided the corporal after a moment. "All right, Molly Pitcher, come on!"

Mary had watched her husband doing his work at the cannon and had learned what to do. At Corporal Pell's commands she swabbed out the cannon barrel and rammed in the powder and ball. She and the men of the crew worked together, keeping the cannon firing steadily all through the long, sizzling hot afternoon.

The British made three attacks against General Anthony Wayne's men. All three were beaten back. As twilight closed over the battlefield, the noise of muskets and cannons died away.

The British attempt to shatter the American army had failed. The British had fought bravely, as they usually did, but the Americans had stood up to them on equal terms for the first time. Rather than continue the battle in the morning, the British army marched away during the night.

The American artillery—the cannons—had played a big part in the American victory. And "Molly Pitcher's" cannon had done its bit because of her. She had shown that a woman could fight as well as a man in the war for America's liberty.

From a victory to a holiday

The Battle of Puebla
Mexico, May 5, 1862

Juan (hwahn) gripped his musket and peered over the low stone wall that he and the other soldiers had built. Beyond the wall stretched a brown, sunlit plain dotted with a few clumps of trees. A dirt road wound across the plain and vanished in the distance. Before long, an army would march up that road. When it did, the silent, sunny plain would explode into battle!

Juan was a soldier in the army of Mexico. He didn't look much like a soldier, however. Instead of a colorful uniform, he wore the same kind of loose white shirt, baggy white pants, and sandals that Mexican farmers wore. Only Juan's cap

showed that he was a soldier. It was a tall, military cap of black leather. It had a brass ornament on the front and a little red cloth ball at the top.

Many of the other soldiers who crouched behind the wall with Juan didn't even have such a cap. They wore the tall, wide-brimmed farmer's hat known as a *sombrero* (som BRAIR oh). The nation of Mexico was simply too poor to buy uniforms, or even parts of uniforms, for most of its soldiers.

Mexico was in bad trouble. For several years, civil war had raged. The wealthy landowners were on one side and the mostly poor, common people were on the other. The war had finally ended by the beginning of 1861, with the common people winning. But the country was nearly ruined. The government had almost no money.

Unfortunately, the Mexican government owed a lot of money to the governments of several nations. It had borrowed money from Spain, France, and Great Britain. Each year it was supposed to pay back some of the money it owed. But in 1861 there wasn't even enough

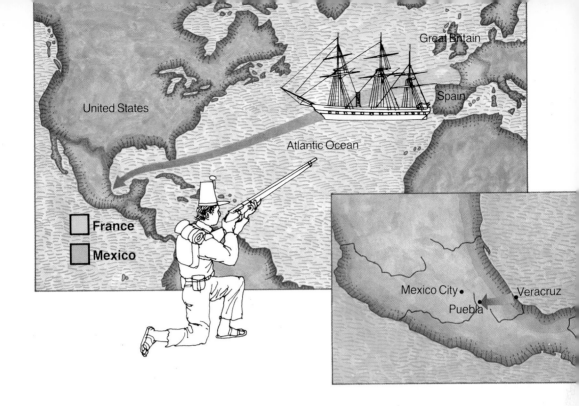

money for things that Mexico needed,
much less to give to other countries. The
Mexican president, Benito Juarez (behn
EE toh HWAR ehz), told the foreign
governments that Mexico couldn't pay
them anything for two years.

The governments of Spain, France, and
Great Britain were outraged by this. They
agreed to work together to force Mexico
to pay its debts. They decided to send a
small army, formed of soldiers from each
of the three nations, to Mexico. This
army was to take over the Mexican port
city of Veracruz (vehr uh KROOZ), where
thousands of ships from all over the
world came to deliver and pick up trade

goods. Each ship paid a tax, which went to the Mexican government. But the foreign army would simply seize all this tax money until it collected enough to pay off Mexico's debts.

Napoleon III

The Spanish and British governments were completely honest about what they intended to do. All they wanted was the money that Mexico owed them. But the French ruler, Emperor Napoleon (nuh POHL yuhn) III, secretly intended to do a great deal more. He had decided that once his soldiers were in Mexico, they should conquer it!

Actually, there were some Mexicans who wanted the French to conquer their country. They were the wealthy landowners, and their followers, who had lost the civil war. They sent word to Napoleon III that if he would help them regain their power, they would help make Mexico into France's greatest friend and ally.

The British, Spanish, and French troops were all in Veracruz by the beginning of 1862. But when the governments of Spain and Great Britain realized what Napoleon III intended to do, they angrily took all their soldiers out of Mexico, leaving the French there alone. In the spring, the small French army of 6,500 men marched out to begin the conquest of the country.

At that time, French soldiers were thought to be the best in the world. French armies had conquered parts of North Africa, the Near East, and Indochina. They had won important victories in a war against Russia in 1855, and against Austria in 1859.

The French army had fine uniforms of dark blue and red. It had many famous

Three famous French regiments took part in the fighting at Puebla. Shown here (from left to right) are a soldier of the Foreign Legion, a Zouave, and one of the *Chasseurs d'Afrique,* or "Hunters of Africa."

regiments, or fighting units. One of these
was the Foreign Legion. This unit of foot
soldiers would fight to the last man and
never surrender. Another famous French
regiment was the Zouaves (zoo AHVZ), also
known for the bravery of its men. They
wore a colorful uniform based on the
clothing of Morocco, with a turban and

wide, baggy red pants. A famous cavalry
regiment was the *Chasseurs d'Afrique*
(shah SOOR da FREEK), or "Hunters of
Africa," renowned for their fearless
charges.

French foot soldiers were armed with a
rifle that could shoot a bullet more than
1,200 yards (1,080 meters). It fired only
one shot at a time, but it could be loaded
quickly and easily. A trained soldier could
fire from three to five times a minute.

However, the leaders of the French
army didn't much believe in a lot of
shooting. A kind of short sword called a
bayonet could be fastened to the barrel of

a rifle. It was used for stabbing an enemy at close range. The French commanders believed that a courageous charge by men using bayonets could win almost any battle.

The first goal of the French army was to capture the Mexican capital, Mexico City. So the French were marching up the road that led to the capital. But,

Both the French and the Mexicans used American Springfield rifles, like the one shown here with a bayonet.

before the road reached Mexico City, it ran through a small city called Puebla (PWEHB lah). And it was at Puebla that the Mexican generals Zaragoza (sahr ah GOH sah) and Diaz (DEE ahs) decided to fight the French.

The Mexican soldiers had fortified Puebla, digging ditches and building low stone walls outside the city. The ditches and the walls would protect them from much of the French fire. And they could shoot at unprotected French soldiers who would be out in the open. Many Mexican soldiers had rather old-fashioned weapons, and the army's cannons were

more than fifty years old. Even so, the
Mexican generals felt their men would do
serious damage to the invaders.

And the Mexican soldiers were grimly
determined to do as much damage as
they could. Most of them were
experienced fighters, who had fought in
the civil war. They had helped defeat the
wealthy landowners, and had helped give
Mexico a government of the common
people. Now, these French invaders were
coming to take away that victory and
make Mexico a servant of the French
Empire. Well, let them try!

Suddenly, Juan leaned forward,
squinting his eyes against the sun's glare.
Surely, that was a cloud of dust he saw,
lying over the road far in the
distance—dust made by the feet of

thousands of men tramping upon
the road's soft, powdery surface.

"They come!" exclaimed Juan.

Others had seen the dust cloud, too. In
the ditches and behind the walls, men
made ready.

The French commander, General Count
Lorencez (law RAHN say), felt nothing but
scorn for the Mexican troops. He was
sure they were far less brave and skillful
than the Russian and Austrian soldiers
the French had beaten. He had no doubt
that his soldiers would so terrify the
Mexicans they would run away. So, when
Lorencez felt he was close enough, he
ordered his army to charge.

Lines of French soldiers trotted
forward. They, too, were sure they could
make the Mexicans run. They held their

rifles like spears. The bayonets, pointing
forward, gleamed in the sunshine. This
sight would certainly strike terror into
the hearts of the Mexicans.

With a crackle that quickly became a
steady, throbbing roar, the Mexican
soldiers opened fire. French soldiers
began to fall by the dozens. The rest kept
on coming. More and more went down.

The French drew closer and closer to
the ditches and the walls. Surely, they
thought, the Mexicans must be getting

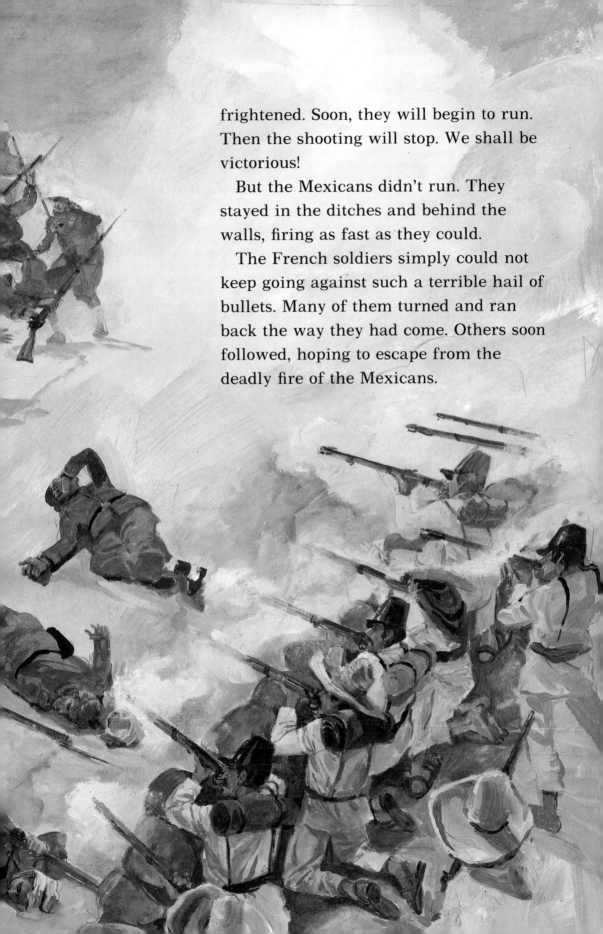

frightened. Soon, they will begin to run. Then the shooting will stop. We shall be victorious!

But the Mexicans didn't run. They stayed in the ditches and behind the walls, firing as fast as they could.

The French soldiers simply could not keep going against such a terrible hail of bullets. Many of them turned and ran back the way they had come. Others soon followed, hoping to escape from the deadly fire of the Mexicans.

French officers managed to stop most of the fleeing soldiers. They formed them into lines again and sent them forward to attack. But the same thing happened! Hundreds were shot down, and the rest came running back!

Again and again, the French commander sent his men forward against the ditches and walls. None of the Frenchmen reached them. The Mexican soldiers were not terrified by the sight of the glittering French bayonets. They did not care that the French were supposed to be the best soldiers in the world. They simply stayed where they were and shot and shot and shot.

By late afternoon, General Count Lorencez realized that his soldiers could not push the Mexicans out of Puebla. Of the 6,500 French soldiers that had begun the battle, more than 1,000 had been shot down. The famous French bayonet charge, which had beaten Russians, Austrians, and others, had not beaten the soldiers of Mexico. Instead, the French were beaten!

Bugles began to sound the call to retreat. Soon, the French army was marching back the way it had come.

a *Cinco de Mayo* celebration in Denver, Colorado

Juan and many of the Mexican soldiers cheered to see the French leave.

The Battle of Puebla did not end the French attempt to conquer Mexico. Enraged by the defeat, Napoleon III sent 30,000 more soldiers to Mexico. It took several more years, and help from the United States, before the French were finally forced to leave Mexico.

Mexico has never forgotten how its army, fighting for freedom, defeated the soldiers that were said to be the best in the world. The Mexican victory at Puebla became a national holiday. Known as *Cinco de Mayo* (SEEN koh deh MAH yoh), or "Fifth of May," it is celebrated by Mexicans everywhere.

Spears against bullets

The Battle of Isandhlwana
South Africa
January 22, 1879

Uguku (oo GOO koo) ran steadily, his bare feet thumping on the dry, hard ground. On his left arm he carried his big war shield of oxhide. In his right hand he carried a cluster of short spears with iron points. All around him, in long lines, were twenty thousand other men with spears and shields, all running. This was an *impi* (IHM pee)—an army of the Zulu (ZOO loo) nation—searching for the enemies that had invaded the land!

The people known as Zulus lived in what is now the province of Natal (nuh TAHL) in the nation of South Africa. But in the year 1879 they were

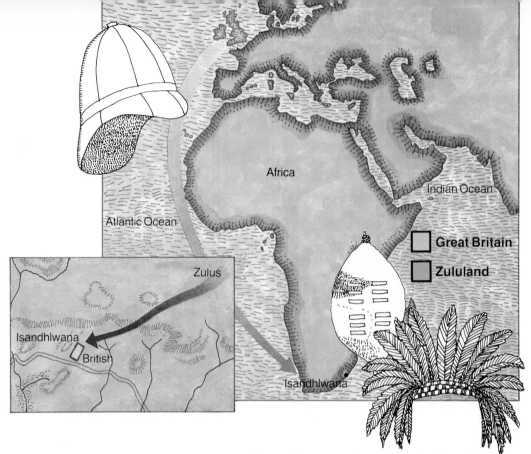

Africa

Indian Ocean

Atlantic Ocean

Zulus

□ **Great Britain**

□ **Zululand**

Isandhlwana

British

Isandhlwana

not part of another nation—their land was free. They lived in small villages scattered about the country, and made their living by herding cattle and farming. They were ruled by a king named Cetshwayo (seht shuh WAY oh).

In most ways, the Zulus were much like the other African people in the lands around them. But in one way they were very different—a way that made them feared by their neighbors. The Zulus were fierce warriors, and were organized into a powerful army.

When Uguku was a young teen-ager, he and about one hundred other boys his age, from his part of the country, were

put into a group called an *Intanga* (ihn
TAN guh). They were led by an older boy
known as an *Induna* (ihn DOO nuh), or
commander. The boys began to learn how
to obey commands, and how to use and
care for weapons.

When Uguku and the others were about
twenty years old, their *Intanga* joined
nine others, all with men their own age,
to form a regiment, a fighting force of the
army. Each young warrior was given a
big oxhide war shield. Its color, all black
with a double row of small white bars
running down the middle, told everyone
what regiment the young warrior
belonged to.

a Zulu warrior in full battle dress

Uguku and the others were also given some throwing spears and a stabbing spear. They learned to use these weapons in the Zulu way. A Zulu regiment would charge close to its foe and quickly throw a shower of spears. Then the warriors would charge straight in to use their stabbing spears up close. Zulu warriors became so skillful at handling their spears that they could even shave and cut their hair with them.

The warriors learned to obey instantly the commands of the *Induna* who led the regiment. Commands were never shouted or spoken, but always given by hand signals. The men of the regiment could run fifty miles (80 kilometers) without stopping, and could go for a long time without food. They were absolutely fearless, because they didn't care if they were killed in a battle. They believed that they would then go straight to heaven.

And so, Uguku, like all the other men in the Zulu army, had become a perfect warrior. He had waited and waited for the chance to fight in a battle. Now, at last, he was going to fight in his first battle. And it would be against the enemies who had invaded his land!

a Zulu shield and spears from 1879

He really didn't know much about these enemies, except that unlike the Zulus, who fought with spears, these enemy warriors had rifles. They were white-skinned men and served a queen who lived far across a great body of water. Uguku didn't know why she had sent her men to invade his country, but she would be sorry she had done so! The *impi* of which his regiment was a part would soon locate these enemy soldiers and destroy them!

The enemies who had invaded Zululand in 1879 were soldiers of the British Empire, which was ruled by Queen Victoria. The British government had decided that the Zulus, with their powerful army, were a danger to British settlers in nearby lands. So, a small British army had been sent to conquer Zululand. The British intended to break up the Zulu army and force King Cetshwayo to rule the country as *they* thought best.

In 1879, the British Army was equipped with a single-shot rifle. Even so, a trained soldier could fire his rifle about six times a minute

In 1879, the British Army was probably the best army in the world. Its foot soldiers were organized in groups of about one thousand men, called battalions. British soldiers wore a red jacket and dark blue trousers tucked into short, black leather boots. In Africa, they wore a light helmet made of cork and covered with white canvas to protect their heads from the hot sun. Each battalion had a number and a special color that appeared on the collar and cuffs of the red jacket.

British soldiers were armed with a rifle that fired one shot at a time for a distance of more than a thousand yards (900 meters). To fire his rifle, a soldier pushed a small lever with his thumb. This opened up the back end of the rifle barrel, called the breech. He put a bullet into place, then lifted the lever to close the breech. He then put the rifle to his shoulder and pulled the trigger.

Each time a man fired, he had to reach into a pouch on his belt for another bullet. An experienced soldier could fire about six times a minute. Each soldier carried a total of seventy bullets in his belt pouches.

These British soldiers from a Royal Artillery battery posed for this photograph while on duty in Zululand.

The British army that marched into Zululand was made up of about five thousand British soldiers and eight thousand African soldiers. The Africans had been trained and given weapons and uniforms by the British.

Although the British leaders knew that the whole Zulu army had more than forty thousand men, they were confident they could win any battle with the Zulus. They did not think spears could beat bullets. The British commander even divided his little army into several parts, or "columns," in order to search in several different directions for the Zulus.

One evening, one of the British columns made camp near the foot of a rocky hill called Isandhlwana (ee sahnd LWAH nuh). The name means "the place like the stomach of an ox." It was toward this same hill that Uguku and the Zulu *impi*—twenty thousand strong—were headed. On the same day the British made camp, the Zulus encamped in a deep valley about five miles from the hill. That night, the Zulu commanders watched the distant, flickering campfires of the British and planned their attack.

Morning came—the morning of January 22, 1879. The commander of the British column took about half his four thousand soldiers and marched off to look for the Zulus. But the direction he took led away from the Zulu camp. This left only about eighteen hundred soldiers in the camp by Isandhlwana. A few horsemen were sent out to search for any sign of Zulus nearby.

The warriors of the Zulu *impi* sat silently in rows in the little valley. Their

commander, Tshingowayo (shihn goh
WAY oh), had decided not to attack until
the next day. So, men had been sent out
to get food for the *impi*.

Uguku, seated halfway up the side of
one of the hills that rose above the valley,
happened to glance up. Instantly, he gave
a shout, and pointed. At the top of the hill
a uniformed man on a horse stared down

at the thousands of Zulu warriors. A
British soldier! The *impi* had been found!

At Uguku's shout, many other warriors
looked up and saw the enemy soldier. At
once, everyone realized the battle must be
fought *now*. Silently, the Zulu warriors
swarmed up the hillside. Reaching the
top, they began to run toward the British
camp in the distance.

They did not run in a mixed-up crowd,
but quickly formed the Zulu battle
formation known as the "charging
buffalo." The men were spread out in a

long line that was about two miles (3 km)
across. On the left and on the right,
thousands of men formed a great curve
that represented the horns of the buffalo.
In the center, where Uguku was, many
rows of warriors represented the buffalo's
body. The "horns" would curl around the
enemy force and push it into the "body,"
where it would be destroyed!

British scouts were now galloping into
their camp with word that the Zulu *impi*
was coming. Bugles sounded the call that
told the soldiers to grab their rifles and
get ready to fight. Officers yelled orders to
their men, telling them what to do.

Most of the British soldiers were veterans—men who had fought in a number of battles. They knew what they had to do, and were not much afraid or excited. Quickly, they formed into lines facing the oncoming Zulus. Even though they saw they were badly outnumbered, they were not worried. They felt they would simply shoot down most of the Zulus before the warriors could reach them.

And it looked as if that was exactly what would happen. As the Zulus came within rifle range, the British and African soldiers began to fire. Kneeling and lying down, to make it harder for thrown spears to hit them, they fired as fast and as carefully as they could. With nearly two thousand men firing several times a minute, the air was filled with a hail of bullets. The sound of the shots was like a never-ending crackle of thunder.

All across the long line of the *impi*, charging warriors began to go down. As the *impi* got to within a few hundred yards (meters) of the British soldiers, Zulus fell by the hundreds! The warriors

realized they could not keep going
against such a storm of bullets—they
would all be killed. They dropped flat to
the ground, so they would be harder to
hit, and began to crawl toward the British.

The British soldiers kept shooting.
Although they could not see the Zulus
hidden in the tall grass, the soldiers had
a good idea where the warriors were.
They shot low, to send their bullets into
the men crawling on the ground.

From time to time, some of the Zulus leaped up and tried to charge at a run. They were instantly shot down. Uguku lay flat, his shield pulled over his body, slowly wiggling his way forward. He heard bullets buzzing over his head. He was angry and grieving that he could not get close to the red-coated invaders to fight them face to face.

By now many of the British soldiers had fired most of the bullets from their

belt pouches. They needed more ammunition to keep up the steady fire that had stopped the Zulus. Officers in charge of each group of soldiers sent men to the wagons for more ammunition.

These men suddenly found that there was a serious problem. The extra ammunition was kept in long wooden boxes, each of which held six hundred bullets. The lids of the boxes were screwed on with nine thick screws. It took two men with screwdrivers several minutes just to open up one box. And as men arrived at the wagons to get more bullets, they discovered that there were only two screwdrivers! Although there was plenty of ammunition—fifty boxes—the men couldn't get the boxes open fast enough.

So, the British and African soldiers began to run out of bullets. Slowly, the steady rattle of rifle fire died away. Soon, only single shots were heard here and there.

The Zulus realized that the terrible hail of bullets had ended. Cautiously, Uguku rose to his feet. All around him, other warriors also stood up. Slowly, they began to move forward.

Nothing happened! No longer did hundreds of bullets come buzzing to cut them down. In delight, Uguku and the others pounded their shields with the ends of their spears, making a sound like thousands of drums. Then, yelling their war cry, and hurling their throwing spears, the Zulus charged!

The British soldiers fought as best they could. Some swung their rifles like clubs. Those who had attached their bayonets to the ends of their rifles tried to stab charging warriors. But the British were vastly outnumbered. Now the Zulus, with their shields and spears, had the advantage. A Zulu warrior could knock a British soldier's bayonet aside with his shield and stab the soldier with his spear!

Soon, it was all over. Some of the British and African soldiers managed to get away on horseback. All the rest—more than twelve hundred men—were killed. The Zulu *impi* had lost three thousand warriors. It was a terrible, bloody battle for both sides. But it was a great victory for the Zulus. They had beaten the invaders!

Sadly, even though the Zulus had won

A photograph of the battlefield at Isandhlwana, taken shortly after the end of the battle.

the Battle of Isandhlwana, they did not keep their freedom. A bigger British army was sent to Zululand. And in a terrible battle near the home of King Cetshwayo, the British badly defeated the Zulus. After that, Zululand was governed by the British. In time, it became part of the nation of South Africa.

There is no monument on the battlefield of Isandhlwana. But there is one on the battlefield where the Zulu warriors were defeated. It says:

IN MEMORY OF THE BRAVE WARRIORS
WHO FELL HERE IN 1879
IN DEFENSE OF THE OLD ZULU ORDER

The Zulu warriors fought bravely for their land's freedom—and lost. Spears could not beat bullets.

The Miracle of the Vistula

The Battle of Warsaw
Poland, August 16-25, 1920

It was a warm August night in the city of Warsaw, capital of Poland. The year was 1920. A man stood looking down at a table spread with maps and sheets of paper. He was a fierce-eyed man, with a big mustache. His name was Józef Pilsudski (yoo zehf peel soot skee), and he was the leader of the Polish nation and the commander of the Polish Army. He was trying to think of a way to save his country.

For a Russian Army was marching through Poland, headed for Warsaw. Polish forces were retreating before the Russians, unable to hold them back. All around Warsaw, men were digging

245

trenches and putting up barbed-wire fences, making ready for the battle that would take place when the Russian Army arrived. Office workers, factory workers, truckdrivers, and businessmen alike prepared to fight to defend the city. If the Russians captured Warsaw, it would be the end. Poland would have to surrender, and once again the Polish people would be ruled by a foreign nation.

At one time, long ago, Poland was a great power—an empire that covered much of central Europe and a large part of what is now Russia. But slowly, it grew weak. In the 1700's it was conquered and divided up. Part was taken by Austria, part by Russia, and part by the German kingdom of Prussia. Poland no longer existed as a nation.

All through the 1800's Austria, Russia, and Prussia ruled Poland. At times, Poles in the Prussian and Russian parts weren't even allowed to speak their own language—they had to speak German or Russian. They were told to forget their history and to forget there had ever been a country called Poland. They weren't to think of themselves as Polish any

During the 1800's, fierce, hard-riding cavalrymen known as Cossacks (KAHS aks) formed special units of the Russian Army.

more—they were Prussians, or Russians, or Austrians.

But most Polish people refused to forget that Poland had once been a great and free nation with its own laws and ruler. Parents secretly told their children about Poland's past so it wouldn't be forgotten. Many Poles dreamed of a day when Poland would be united again as a free land. Several times, people in each of the three parts had tried to revolt and break free from the country that ruled them. But the revolutions failed, and thousands of Poles were killed or imprisoned.

Then, in the early 1900's, there was a sudden, tremendous change! It was the year 1918 and World War I had been raging for four years. The three nations that ruled Poland were in serious trouble.

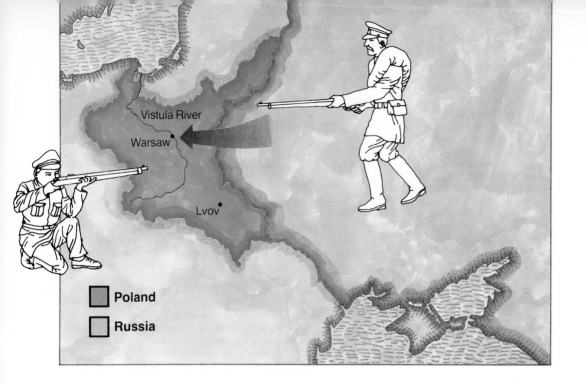

First, the Russians were pushed out of
their part of Poland by the German
Army. Next, Austria surrendered to its
enemies. When its army broke up, the
people in the part of Poland ruled by
Austria suddenly found themselves free.
And, finally, facing defeat and civil war,
Germany took all of its troops out of the
German part of Poland. All three parts of
Poland were free for the first time in
more than 125 years!

Quickly, the Polish leaders from the
three sections held a meeting. They
declared to the world that Poland was
now a single independent nation. They
appointed Józef Pilsudski as the first head
of the government. Pilsudski had worked

for years to make Poland a free nation, and was a hero to most Polish people.

But the new nation quickly learned that it would have to fight to stay free. In Russia there had been a civil war that brought down the government of the old Russian Empire. Now, the new government, under the control of the Communist (KAHM yuh nihst) Party, had sent an army to recapture the part of Poland that had belonged to the old Russian Empire!

The Russian Army was about 200,000 strong. The Polish army formed to stop it was only about 120,000 strong. The men in both armies looked more like tramps or scarecrows than soldiers. War had raged in both countries for years. There were shortages of food, clothing, and many other things. Most of the soldiers wore old, ragged uniforms. Many Polish soldiers did not even have shoes.

The men of both armies were armed with rifles that could fire five bullets, one after another, before they had to be reloaded. Each army also had many machine guns, and cannons that could fire explosive shells about three miles (5

Polish soldiers struggle to move their horse-drawn artillery as they march to meet the Russian Army.

kilometers). There were also a few armored cars on each side.

Józef Pilsudski's face was grim as he looked at the maps and reports that showed what was happening. The Polish Army was stretched out in a long line from Warsaw to the city of Lvov (luh VAWF), nearly two hundred miles (320 km) away. The Russian Army was stretched out over the same distance. Slowly, the center of the Polish line was being pushed back, and a very strong Russian force was moving steadily toward Warsaw.

Pilsudski knew that if Warsaw were taken, Poland would lose the war. It

Russian machine gunners

bothered him that one of the strongest parts of the Polish Army had to be tied down at Warsaw, doing nothing until the Russians arrived. Pilsudski wanted to attack and push the Russians back, but he did not dare move the troops out of Warsaw.

Then, suddenly, he saw the answer! A bold, daring plan flashed into his mind. It would be dangerous, but if it worked, Warsaw—and Poland—would be saved!

Quickly, Pilsudski began writing orders for the commanders of Polish Army

units. Commanders of troops in the middle of the Polish line were told to pull their men back and gather together near a city called Deblin (DEH bleen), about halfway between Warsaw and Lvov. The troops in Warsaw were told to hold on against the Russian attack, and be ready to make an attack of their own when Pilsudski gave the order.

Pilsudski drove to Deblin to take personal command of the special force he had built up there. It made him sad to see how poorly clothed and equipped the Polish soldiers were. He later wrote that he had "never seen such ragamuffins." He went among the men, talking to them, doing his best to make them feel confident they could beat the Russians.

Meanwhile, the Russian Army moved

steadily toward Warsaw. The troops at the far right of the long line swept around the northern side of the city to come at it from behind. The rest of the Russian right side began to cross the bridge over the Vistula (VIHS choo luh) River leading into Warsaw. The Russian soldiers ran into heavy machine-gun and rifle fire from the Polish troops defending the city. A fierce battle began.

The middle of the Russian line turned toward the north, to hurry to Warsaw and help the Russian soldiers fighting there. The left part of the Russian line continued straight on toward the city of Lvov. Thus, a big gap began to open up between what had been the left and the middle.

At that moment, Józef Pilsudski struck! He ordered his little army at Deblin to attack. Because the middle of the Russian line had moved past Deblin, the Poles now hit the enemy from behind!

The attack caught the Russians, marching toward Warsaw, by complete surprise. They heard the sudden rumble of cannons and the whine of shells slicing through the air. The road exploded with great bursts of whirling

smoke and dust as the shells struck. The marchers quickly ran to the sides of the road, seeking ditches and other places where they could hide from the deadly rain of shells. But then, Polish soldiers, hidden among trees along the road, began to fire at them. The chat-chat-chat of machine guns and the crack of thousands of rifles made a deafening sound.

The Russian soldiers had thought that part of their own army was marching behind them. Now they realized they were about to be surrounded by enemy soldiers. They became panic-stricken. By the thousands they ran, toward the north and the east, away from the Poles who were closing in from the south and west. The ragged, barefoot Polish soldiers moved grimly after them, determined to chase them right out of Poland!

Pilsudski now drove to Warsaw. It was a dangerous trip because the countryside was swarming with Russian foot soldiers and cavalry. As his car entered Warsaw from the south, Pilsudski could hear the sounds of battle coming from the eastern part of the city. The Polish defenders of Warsaw were managing to keep the

Russians out, as Pilsudski had hoped they would.

Pilsudski now gave a new order. No longer would the Polish soldiers simply hold off the attackers. Now they were to attack and push the Russians back.

It seemed impossible to carry out such an order. The Polish soldiers were badly outnumbered. Even so, many of them began to move forward. They crawled with their heads down, trying to keep from being hit by bullets. When they found places to hide, they would stop to shoot at the Russians. While some did this, others kept crawling closer.

The Russian commanders realized that the Poles were suddenly advancing against them. And they now learned that the Russian force they had thought was coming up from the south to help them had been destroyed! Instead, a Polish force was coming at them from that direction. The Russians realized they were in a trap—Polish soldiers were moving against them from two directions!

Now this part of the Russian Army began to collapse as the other part had. Russian soldiers ran for their lives, leaving behind supply carts, ammunition wagons, cannons, and machine guns. The whole Polish countryside was filled with mobs of men heading for the Russian border.

Józef Pilsudski had launched his attacks on August 16, and by August 25, the Russian Army that had come into Poland was no more. Pilsudski's Polish Army captured 66,000 Russian prisoners, 231 cannons, 1,023 machine guns, and thousands of carts and wagons. The victory that came when the Polish soldiers in Warsaw pushed the Russian army back across the Vistula River became known as the miracle of the Vistula. In just ten days, Poland had changed from a country that was nearly beaten to one that was victorious—and still free!

The battle for the sky

The Battle of Britain
July 10-October 31, 1940

Weeping mothers kissed their children good-by and watched as buses carried them to safety in the country. People covered the windows of their houses with heavy curtains, bought fire extinguishers, and piled sandbags for protection. In museums, they took down works of art and valuable displays and stored them far underground. The cities of Great Britain faced destruction. The people did what they could to protect their children, their houses, their places of work, and their nation's treasures.

It was 1940, the first full year of World War II. The armies of Nazi (NAHT see)

As the bombing began, English children in London were sent to the country where they would be safer.

Germany had swept across Europe, conquering Poland, Norway, Denmark, Belgium, Holland, and finally, France. Now, Great Britain stood alone, knowing that it would be next to face the conquering German attack. And that attack would begin with an onslaught from the sky by planes of the *Luftwaffe* (LUFT vahf uh), the German air force.

There were two main kinds of war planes at this time, bombers and fighters. Bombers were big heavy planes with from two to four engines and crews of five or six men. Their job was to damage or destroy factories, bridges, airfields, or anything else that was useful to the enemy. Fighter planes were smaller and faster, with only one engine and one person in them. Their job was to shoot down enemy airplanes. Although all these planes were propeller-driven, they could move at speeds between two hundred and three hundred miles per hour (320-480 kilometers per hour). They were armed with many machine guns, and some fighter planes also had a small cannon.

The British knew that the *Luftwaffe* would try to "soften them up." The Germans would bomb them mercilessly in an attempt to make Great Britain surrender. But first, the Germans had to wipe out Britain's Royal Air Force, the RAF, to make it easier for the German Army to invade England.

These British airplane spotters are working on a London rooftop during an air raid.

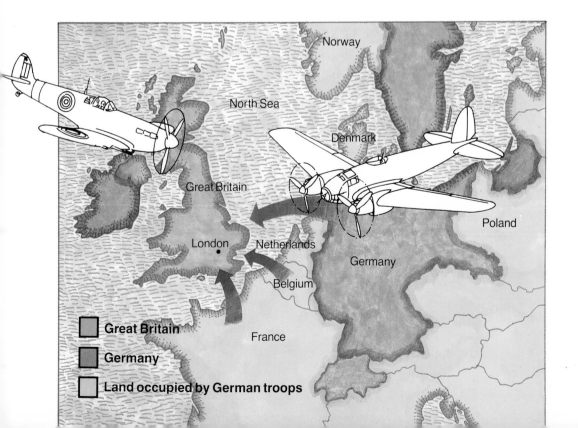

Norway

North Sea

Denmark

Great Britain

Poland

London

Netherlands

Germany

Belgium

France

☐ Great Britain

☐ Germany

☐ Land occupied by German troops

To fight off this air attack, the British depended on three main things. First, there were the radar stations located at spots along the English coast. With their electronic screens, these stations could see enemy airplanes coming long before they reached the coast, and could quickly give an alarm.

Second, there were the fighter planes of the RAF. When the call came from a radar station, squadrons of fighters would roar into the sky to attack the German bombers.

The German Heinkel was a twin-engine heavy bomber.

Third, there were the antiaircraft guns—cannons that fired exploding shells high into the sky. These guns could fire steadily, many times a minute, and just a few of them could fill the sky with explosions. The exploding shells hurled many sharp pieces of metal in all directions. For an airplane, this was like flying through a deadly rain. The metal pieces could slice through a plane's body, causing damage and killing or injuring the plane's crew. And if a shell exploded close enough to a plane, it could destroy it.

The Spitfire was one of Britain's best fighter aircraft.

However, it would not be easy for the British to fight off the air attack. For one thing, they were outnumbered almost two-to-one. They had about 700 fighter planes, but the German air force had 1,500 long-range bombers and 1,100 fighters. The bombers were armed with many machine guns, and were well able to defend themselves. The fighter planes that flew with them would also protect them. And some of the British planes were not as fast or as good as most of the German fighter planes.

The British also had the disadvantage of not knowing where the Germans would strike. So, they had to place

A radar antenna of the kind the British used to locate German aircraft.

squadrons, or groups, of fighters, all over the country. This way, they could fight off German planes no matter where they attacked. But this meant that if the Germans attacked in the north, many of the British planes in the south would be too far away to be of any help. Thus, the Germans could put all their force in one place, but the British couldn't.

The British also didn't have nearly enough antiaircraft guns—only about two thousand. They had to split these up into many small groups in order to defend the main cities, airfields, and other places that might be attacked.

But, difficulties or not, the British knew they had to win the coming battle in the sky. If the German bombers destroyed many of the factories that made weapons, Great Britain would soon be unable to fight. If the Germans wiped out the RAF, as they hoped to do, the German Army could invade Great Britain much more easily.

And Great Britain had to fight off the invasion. If the British people were conquered, they would lose their freedom forever! The leaders of Germany—the Nazis—intended to conquer the world, to kill many people and make the rest slaves! If Great Britain were conquered, life would be dreadful for most of its people!

Adolf Hitler was the leader of Nazi Germany.

So, the people of Great Britain hurried to strengthen their defenses as much as they could before the *Luftwaffe* launched its attack. They had only a few weeks after France surrendered to Germany on June 22. On July 10, small groups of German planes made quick raids. Then, on August 12, the *Luftwaffe* struck with full force.

It was a gray, cloudy day. Hundreds of German bombers and fighters roared over the white cliffs of the English coast. Breaking into small groups, they headed

Winston Churchill was Great Britain's leader.

toward airfields and radar stations along the coast. From nearby airfields, British fighter planes sped up to meet them.

The British pilots tried to get to the bombers, to shoot them down before they could drop their bombs. The German fighter planes tried to protect the bombers by forcing the British planes to fight them instead. "Dogfights" broke out, with pairs of fighter planes turning, twisting, looping, and veering to try to keep from being hit by an enemy's bullets. All the while, each pilot tried to get into a position to shoot at an enemy plane.

Meanwhile, the bombers droned steadily on, their pilots determined to get to the places they had been ordered to bomb. If a bomber was attacked, it fought back. Machine gunners in the tail and on the sides fired back at attacking planes, while the pilot kept flying steadily toward the target. The bombers also had to fly through bursts of antiaircraft shells.

On this first full day of the attack, victory went to the British. While the Germans bombed six radar stations, only one was so badly damaged it couldn't keep operating. The RAF lost 22 planes, but 31 German planes were destroyed.

The next day, things went even worse for the Germans. There were hundreds of attacks by groups of German planes, but most were fought off. The *Luftwaffe* lost

Even very young children had to practice wearing gas masks because of the fear of a gas attack.

45 planes, the British lost only 13. And by the end of another five days, after thousands of attacks both day and night, the Germans had lost 363 planes to 211 for the British.

But even though the *Luftwaffe* had lost 152 more planes than the RAF, Great Britain was growing weaker. Factories that made the British fighter planes had been bombed, and there were only 171 new planes to replace the 211 lost! It took a long time to train new pilots, and there were only 63 men to replace the 154 fighter pilots who had been killed. And these new pilots weren't yet as skilled as the others had been.

The commanders of the German air force knew that despite their own losses, they were weakening the British. They began to attack harder. They made bigger attacks on factories making the British fighter planes, and on the airfields where the fighter planes were kept. Every day for the next two weeks, hundreds of German planes—sometimes as many as 1,500—came roaring over England.

The British fighter pilots knew that everything depended on them. Each day

Londoners spent many nights sleeping in subway stations during bombing attacks.

they faced death several times, racing up into the sky to fight off the terrible attacks. They had time only to snatch a few hours sleep and gobble down a hurried meal. Then they were fighting again.

Things began to look worse. During the two weeks of the attacks, the British destroyed 380 German planes, but lost 286 planes and 103 pilots. Another 128 pilots were injured and unable to fly. The RAF was beating the *Luftwaffe*, but it was losing the battle. It would soon be too weak to fight anymore!

But the Germans, too, were worried. They had lost a great many planes, but still hadn't wiped out the British fighter planes. They felt they must do something to make the British use up fighter planes more quickly. So, they decided to do what the British people had feared all along—attack the cities of Great Britain, and especially the city of London. They knew the RAF would use all the planes it had to defend the nation's capital.

In the late afternoon of September 7, 300 German bombers and 600 fighters droned toward London. Throughout the city, sirens began to make the terrifying, deep wailing sound that warned of an air raid. People ran for shelter in the basements of buildings and in the subway stations. From airfields all around, British fighters rose into the air to defend London. Antiaircraft guns around the city began to spit explosions into the sky.

Bombs exploded throughout the city—CR-UMP! CR-UMP! Soon, warehouses along the river that runs through London were burning fiercely. When the bombers finished their task and turned away, London firemen began the work of putting out the fires. People started digging into piles of broken brick and stone, searching for the dead and injured.

That same night, the air raid sirens wailed again as 250 more German bombers flew over the city. By morning there were more fires and more piles of broken stone that had once been buildings. And the next day, the bombers came again.

The British knew that the invasion of their country was going to come at any moment. Pilots of British scout planes spotted more and more boats and ships in

German bombers
totally destroyed this
famous cathedral in
the city of Coventry,
which is northwest of
London.

the French ports across from England. The fact was, the Nazi leader, Adolf Hitler, had ordered the German Army and Navy to invade England on September 21—two weeks away!

Day after day, night after night, flights of German bombers and fighters roared over London. And during many of these raids, more British planes were shot down than German ones! The RAF grew steadily weaker. In addition, hundreds of London's citizens were killed, and thousands injured.

But the British struck back in other ways. British bombers began to attack the German ships getting ready for the invasion. Many were damaged or destroyed.

On September 15, the *Luftwaffe* launched an attack to finally wipe out the

last of the British fighter planes. During the day, 230 bombers and 700 fighters, in several groups, sped toward London.

But the British radar stations saw all these attacks coming and gave the alarm in plenty of time. The RAF Fighter Command sent up almost every plane it had. As the German planes roared across England, they found themselves under constant attack from squadron after squadron of British fighters!

A British squadron would rush to attack and fight as long as it could. Then it would race back to its airfield for more fuel and ammunition—and go up to fight again. The pilots went without food and sleep. Each man was doing the job of three or four. They made it seem as if the RAF had far more planes than it really did.

And they won the battle! Under such steady attack, many German bombers turned back rather than take a chance on being destroyed. Many others were shot down. Very few got to London, and their bombs did little damage. By the end of the day, the RAF had lost 26 planes, but the *Luftwaffe* had lost 60! This was the worst loss the Germans had ever taken.

In the German capital, Berlin, the

**The markings on this RAF pilot's plane show
that he has shot down ten enemy aircraft.**

commanders of the German army, navy, and air force met to discuss what to do. British bombing raids had badly damaged the invasion fleet. And it looked as if the RAF still had plenty of planes with which to fight off an invasion. The German generals and admirals decided it would be much too dangerous to try to make the invasion now. They urged the Nazi leader, Adolf Hitler, to call it off.

The *Luftwaffe* continued to make air raids on England and parts of Scotland and Northern Ireland. The people of Great Britain continued to live with fear and grief for a long time. But now they knew there would be no invasion. Just as their seamen had stopped the Spanish Armada in 1588, their airmen had now stopped the Germans in 1940. A few hundred men of the RAF, risking death every day—and often several times a day—had kept Great Britain free!

Speaking of these men, the British leader Winston Churchill said that never had so many people owed so much to so few. The millions of people of Great Britain owed their freedom to those few hundred brave fighter pilots.

Books to Read

There are many good books about important wars, famous battles, and heroes and heroines of military history. A few are listed here. Your school or public library will have some of these, as well as many others.

Ages 7 to 9

Civil War Paper Soldiers in Full Color by A. G. Smith (Dover, 1985)
Union and Confederate soldiers of the American Civil War are printed on glossy cardboard pages. These may be cut out and mounted to make dioramas or to play war games.

Knights and Armor Coloring Book by A. G. Smith (Dover, 1985)
This book provides historically accurate outline drawings of armored knights from several periods of history in which knights played the main role in warfare.

Knights and Castles by Jonathan Rutland (Random House, 1987)
The story of the way of life of the fighting men known as knights, illustrated with many exciting full-color pictures.

Molly Pitcher, Young Patriot by Augusta Stevenson (Aladdin Books, 1986)
The story of the childhood of Mary Hays, who became famous as Molly Pitcher, a heroine of the American Revolution.

War and Weapons by Brian Williams (Random House, 1987)
This is a pictorial presentation of how war is fought at the present time and how the weapons of war perform and are used.

Ages 10 to 12

The Alamo by Leonard Everett Fisher (Holiday House, 1987)
The author tells the story of the tiny building that became a fortress during the famous battle in the war Texas fought to gain freedom from Mexico.

The Battle of Britain by Julia Markl (Franklin Watts, 1984)
Here is a vivid description of the air battle in which a small number of British fighter pilots saved their nation from invasion and conquest.

Children of the Book by Peter Carter (Oxford University Press, 1984)
This prize-winning book from England tells about the invasion of Austria by the Turks in 1683, and the siege of Vienna.

1812: The War Nobody Won by
Albert Marrin (Atheneum, 1985)
Illustrations, maps, diagrams, and
interesting text tell the story of the
war sometimes known as America's
second war for independence.

Famous Air Force Bombers by
George Sullivan (Dodd, Mead, 1985)
Famous Air Force Fighters by George
Sullivan (Dodd, Mead, 1985)
Famous Navy Attack Planes by George
Sullivan (Dodd, Mead, 1986)
Famous Navy Fighter Planes by George
Sullivan (Dodd, Mead, 1986)
These four books provide pictures
and descriptions of the airplanes that
helped to win World War II.

George Midgett's War by Sally
Edwards (Scribner, 1985)
This is the story of how the
American Revolutionary War
affected the people of a fishing
community in North Carolina.

A Roman Soldier by Giovanni Caselli
(Peter Bedrick, 1986)
This is an attractively and
authentically illustrated story of the
life of a young Roman soldier, in
peace and in combat, some eighteen
hundred years ago.

**The Story of Sherman's March to the
Sea** by Zachary Kent (Childrens
Press, 1987)
This book is about one of the major
campaigns of the American Civil
War.

**The Yanks Are Coming: The United
States in the First World War** by
Albert Marrin (Atheneum, 1986)
The part played by American
soldiers and industry in the war that
changed the world.

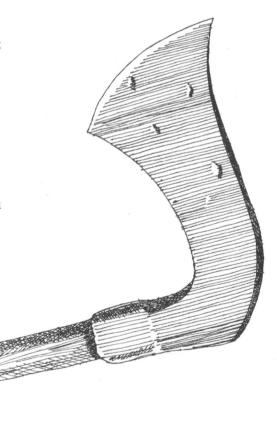

New Words

Here are some of the words you have met in this book. Many of them may be new to you. All are useful words to know. Next to each word, you'll see how to say the word: ambush (AM bush). The part in capital letters is said more loudly than the rest of the word. One or two sentences tell what the word means.

ambush (AM bush)
An ambush is a surprise attack made in a place where soldiers can hide until the enemy arrives.

barbarian (bahr BAIR ee uhn)
A barbarian is a wild, uncivilized person.

battalion (buh TAL yuhn)
A battalion is part of an army. It may be formed of from 500 to 1,000 soldiers and is divided into smaller units called companies.

bayonet (bay uh NEHT)
A bayonet is a kind of short sword that can be attached to the muzzle, or front end, of a rifle or musket.

bombardment (bahm BAHRD mehnt)
A bombardment is steady firing by many cannons at a town or a place occupied by enemy soldiers.

cartridge (KAHR trihj)
A cartridge is a long, round container that holds gunpowder and a bullet. Old-fashioned cartridges were made of paper. Now they are generally made of brass.

crescent (KREHS uhnt)
A crescent is a thin curve, like the shape of a quarter moon or half a circle.

emperor (EHM puhr uhr)
An emperor is the ruler of an empire.

empire (EHM pyr)
An empire is a group of several different countries that are all under one government with one ruler. Each country might have its own king, but the king of one country is the emperor, or ruler, of the empire.

exhaustion (ehg ZAWS chuhn)
Exhaustion is being so tired and worn out that it is impossible to keep going without taking a rest.

formation (fawr MAY shuhn)
A battle formation is the way the soldiers of an army are arranged in order to fight. In the past, this was generally three long rows, one behind the other, or a square formed of many rows close together.

galleon (GAL ee uhn)
A galleon was a large wooden warship with many big square sails. It had high sides and three or four decks, one above the other, with rows of cannons along the sides of each deck.

horde (hawrd)
A horde is an enormous crowd.

Mongol (MAHNG guhl)
A Mongol is an Asian who lives in Mongolia and nearby parts of China and Siberia. About eight hundred years ago, the Mongols conquered much of China, Russia, and other lands and created a gigantic empire.

musket (MUHS kiht)
A musket was the kind of gun used by armies from about 1600 to 1850. It could fire only one shot at a time. It then had to be reloaded, which took some time.

Nazi (NAHT see)

The Nazi party was a political party that governed Germany from 1933 to 1945. Nazis believed that the government should control industry and much of what people did. They also felt that certain groups of people should not be allowed to live. They hoped to gain control of most of the world.

pike (pyk)

A pike was a very long spear and was the main weapon of most European armies from about 1470 to 1690.

quilted jacket (KWIHL tuhd JAK iht)

A quilted jacket for a soldier of long ago was made by sewing two pieces of canvas together with stitches forming rows of squares. The squares were open, like pockets, and a thin piece of metal was put into each before it was sewn shut. Thus, a quilted jacket was a kind of armor.

radar (RAY dahr)

Radar is an electronic instrument that gives off streams of radio waves. If the waves hit something, such as an airplane, they bounce back and cause patterns of light to appear on a kind of television screen. This can show the distance, direction, height, and speed of the airplane. The word *radar* comes from *r*adio *d*etection *a*nd *r*anging.

regiment (REHJ uh muhnt)

A regiment is a unit of an army. It is generally formed of several thousand men and is divided into smaller parts called battalions.

revolt (rih VOHLT)

A revolt is an uprising of people against an unpopular leader, government, or law. Revolts often result in fighting and destruction.

score (skawr)

A score is twenty of something.

shell (shehl)

A cannon shell is a hollow container filled with gunpowder and usually also with pieces of metal. By means of a fuse, the gunpowder is exploded after the shell is fired from the cannon. This causes the pieces of metal to fly through the air.

traitor (TRAY tuhr)

A traitor is a person who works against his own nation, government, or the people who trust him.

turban (TUR buhn)

A turban is a headdress worn by men in parts of North Africa and Asia. It is a scarf that is wound around the head.

typhoon (ty FOON)

A typhoon is a severe hurricane or cyclone that strikes in the western Pacific Ocean, mainly from July to October.

unit (YOO niht)

A unit is any group of soldiers making up part of an army. A unit may have only a few men or many thousands.

veteran (VEHT uhr uhn)

A veteran is a person who has been in an armed force such as an army or navy for a long time. Veterans are an important part of any armed force because they have a great deal of skill and experience.

visor (VY zuhr)

A visor is the movable front part of a helmet, such as those worn by knights. The visor could be raised or lowered to protect the face.

volunteer (vahl uhn TIHR)

A volunteer is a person who joins an armed force by choice rather than by being drafted to serve.

Illustration Acknowledgments

The publishers of *Childcraft* gratefully acknowledge the courtesy of the following photographers, agencies, and organizations for illustrations in this volume. When all the illustrations for a sequence of pages are from a single source, the inclusive page numbers are given. Credits should be read from left to right, top to bottom, on their respective pages. All illustrations are the exclusive property of the publishers of *Childcraft* unless names are marked with an asterisk (*).

Cover: Aristocrat and Standard binding—Isidre Mones
        Discovery binding—Beverly Rich
        Heritage binding—Marcel Miralles; Richard Hook; Marcel Miralles; Bert Dodson; Isidre Mones; Toby Gowing; Arvis Stewart; Robert Korta; Bert Dodson

1–5:	Arvis Stewart
6–7:	George Guzzi
8–9:	Richard Hook
10–11:	George Suyeoka
12–15:	Richard Hook
16–17:	Eric Lessing, Magnum*; George Guzzi
18–19:	George Guzzi; Richard Hook
20–23:	Richard Hook
24–27:	Marcel Miralles
28–29:	George Suyeoka; Ronald Sheridan*
30–31:	Marcel Miralles; British Museum*; Ronald Sheridan*
32–33:	Marcel Miralles; British Museum*
34–35:	Marcel Miralles
36–37:	George Guzzi; The Louvre, Paris*
38–41:	Marcel Miralles
42–43:	Marcel Miralles; Royal Museum of Scotland*
44–49:	Marcel Miralles
50–53:	Fernando Fernandez
54–55:	George Guzzi; George Suyeoka
56–57:	Fernando Fernandez
58–59:	Ronald Sheridan*; Fernando Fernandez
60–61:	Fernando Fernandez
62–63:	George Guzzi
64–69:	Fernando Fernandez
70–71:	Teuto Press for Interfoto*
72–73:	Bert Dodson
74–75:	Bert Dodson; George Suyeoka
76–77:	Bert Dodson
78–79:	Ronald Sheridan*; Claus Hansmann*; Bert Dodson
80–81:	Bert Dodson; George Guzzi
82–83:	Bert Dodson; George Guzzi
84–87:	Bert Dodson
88–89:	Arvis Stewart
90–91:	Shashinka Photo Library*
92–93:	Imperial Household Collection, Kyoto*; George Suyeoka
94–95:	Shashinka Photo Library*
96–97:	Arvis Stewart; George Guzzi
98–100:	Arvis Stewart
102–103:	Artstreet*; Arvis Stewart
104–105:	Arvis Stewart
106–107:	Chris Warner
108–109:	George Suyeoka
110–111:	Chris Warner
112–113:	George Guzzi
114–115:	Chris Warner
116–117:	Schweizerisches Landesmuseum, Zurich*
118–121:	Chris Warner
122–123:	Isidre Mones
124–125:	George Suyeoka; The Louvre, Paris*
126–127:	French Government Tourist Office*; American Numismatic Society*
128–131:	Isidre Mones
132–133:	Metropolitan Museum of Art, Rogers Fund, 1904*; Isidre Mones
134–135:	Roger Roland Fuhr, ROLANDesign*
136–137:	Isidre Mones
138–139:	George Guzzi
140–143:	Isidre Mones
144–145:	Bibliotheque Nationale*; Ronald Sheridan*
146–147:	Lee Boynton
148–149:	Lee Boynton; George Suyeoka
150–151:	Lee Boynton; Bridgeman Art Library from Art Resource*
152–153:	George Guzzi
154–159:	Lee Boynton
160–161:	National Maritime Museum*; Detail of oil on canvas by Daniel Mytens, Granger Collection*; Granger Collection*
162–163:	National Maritime Museum*
164–167:	Lee Boynton
168–169:	Marcel Miralles
170–171:	George Suyeoka
172–173:	Marcel Miralles; George Guzzi
174–175:	Marcel Miralles
176–177:	Detail of an anonymous painting at the Heeresgeschichtliches Museum, Vienna from Hubert Josse*
178–179:	Marcel Miralles
180–181:	Heeresgeschichtliches Museum, Vienna*; Metropolitan Museum of Art*
182–183:	Marcel Miralles
184–185:	Marcel Miralles; George Guzzi
186–187:	Polish Museum of America*
188–191:	Marcel Miralles
192–193:	Toby Gowing
194–195:	Roger Roland Fuhr, ROLANDesign*; Artstreet*
196–197:	George Suyeoka
198–199:	Toby Gowing
200–201:	Monmouth County Historical Association*
202–207:	Toby Gowing
208–209:	Granger Collection*
210–211:	Bert Dodson
212–213:	George Suyeoka
214–215:	Giraudon from Art Resource*; Bert Dodson
216–217:	Roger Roland Fuhr, ROLANDesign*
218–221:	Bert Dodson
222–223:	Lowell Georgia, Photo Researchers*
224–225:	Robert Korta
226–227:	George Suyeoka; Robert Korta
228–229:	George Guzzi; National Army Museum*
230–231:	Robert Korta
232–233:	Africana Museum, Johannesburg*
234–241:	Robert Korta
242–243:	National Army Museum*
244–245:	Richard Hook
246–247:	Polish Museum of America*
248–249:	George Suyeoka
250–251:	Richard Hook; George Guzzi
252–257:	Richard Hook
258–259:	George Guzzi
260–261:	Syndication International from Photo Trends*; Bettmann Archive*; George Suyeoka
262–263:	George Guzzi
264–265:	George Guzzi; Bettmann Archive*; Imperial War Museum*; Winston Churchill Memorial and Library, Westminster College*
266–267:	George Guzzi
268–269:	Popperfoto*
270–271:	George Guzzi; Imperial War Museum*
272–273:	Imperial War Museum*
274–275:	George Guzzi
276–277:	Robert Capa, Magnum*

Index

This index is an alphabetical list of the important topics covered in this book. It will help you find information given in both words *and* pictures. To help you understand what an entry means, there is often a helping word in parentheses. For example, **Aristides** (Greek commander). If there is information in both words and pictures, you will see the words *with pictures* after the page number. If there is *only* a picture, you will see the word *picture* before the page number.